THE WILDERNESS
ROUTE FINDER

THE WILDERNESS ROUTE FINDER

The Classic Guide to Finding Your Way in the Wild

Calvin Rutstrum

Illustrated by Leslie Kouba

University of Minnesota Press

Minneapolis

To my wife, Florence, whose editing and typing of the manuscript have been the toughest orientation job of all.

First University of Minnesota Press edition, 2000

Published by the University of Minnesota Press
111 Third Avenue South, Suite 290
Minneapolis, MN 55401-2520
http://www.upress.umn.edu

A Cataloging-in-Publication record for this book is available from the Library of Congress.

ISBN 978-0-8166-3661-7

Printed on acid-free paper

The University of Minnesota is an equal-opportunity educator and employer.

ACKNOWLEDGMENTS

The author would like to thank the following:

Surveys and Mapping Branch, Department of Mines and Technical Surveys, Ottawa, Ontario, Canada, for the canoe-route map of Lac De Gras;

U. S. Department of Agriculture, Forest Service, Rocky Mountain Region, Denver, Colorado, for the pack-horse-trail map of Maroon Bells-Snowmass Wilderness and the aerial oblique photo of the wild area panorama;

Marble Arms Corp., Gladstone, Michigan, for the photos of the wrist strap, lapel, and the sled, snowshoe and canoe mount compasses;

Eugene Dietzgen Co., Chicago, Illinois, for the photo of the "top-site" transit;

Leupold & Stevens Instruments, Inc., Portland, Oregon, for the photo of the Sportsman Compass;

Keuffel & Esser Co., Hoboken, New Jersey, for the photos of the cruiser's-type compass and the pocket transit, and permission to reproduce the marine-type sextant illustration;

W. & L. E. Gurley, Troy, New York, for the photos of the forester's-type compass and the mountain, or explorer's, transit;

Silva Inc., La Porte, Indiana, for the photo of the Swedish orienteering compass;

Kern Instruments, Inc., Port Chester, New York, for the photo of light, compact, explorer's theodolite;

Taylor Instrument Companies, Rochester, New York, for the photos of the magnetic, open-face, and pocket compasses.

CONTENTS

INTRODUCTION

The purpose of this small volume is to fulfill the outdoorsman's long-felt need for easily understood, practical, graphically illustrated information on how to find his way through wilderness areas.

Route finding has for most been a problem ever since man first sought to move more freely over the earth's surface. Small parties and individuals intent upon recreation, hunting, fishing, research, prospecting, and other pursuits in wilderness areas often find it difficult with limited budgets to hire competent guides and are themselves not always equipped with the special knowledge needed to guide themselves. When there is ample knowledge for free, independent movement of all members of a party in the field of operation, success of a venture generally becomes more promising.

The material in this volume differs from most information on the subject in that it employs direct, step-by-step, nontechnical explanations of procedure, avoiding the heretofore complex academic formulas of basic route-finding principles. The sophisticated will, therefore, excuse the use of such expressions as the sun "traveling along the earth surface" rather than "its angular relationship to the earth in the celestial sphere"—technical language which would perhaps only confuse the layman.

The greater part of the book deals with the prevention of getting lost. It takes up ordinary route-finding procedures in general, using the simple concept of lines of position and other common factors as they relate to both natural and man-made base lines. Since such lines of position, natural or otherwise, are not always available in wilderness areas, short, simple methods that can be understood by all for determining latitude lines of position by convenient sextant sights on the sun and a few well-positioned stars are included. Also, a short meridian-time-sight method for longitude, in preference to the long methods such as H.O. 214 and others, has been included, primarily as a last resort for those occasions when other common factors, usually adequate, fail. Sextants can now be had through government surplus at one-tenth their original cost, providing available equipment for all who care to pursue this subject.

Because the null point of any ordinary portable radio, used with compass and map, can fix a position, a simple form of radio route finding and radio navigation has been included.

C. R.

CHAPTER ONE

Getting Rid of Delusions

PERHAPS the two chief obstacles to route-finding progress for the layman have been the tendency to endow man with a special sense of direction he does not possess and to regard the subject of route finding as beyond the scope of the rank and file. We might do well to dispel both of these notions and try to identify some other common delusions.

Basically, we need to recognize that man cannot walk in a straight line or otherwise maintain a directional course without relying on some tangible clue wholly apart from his own instincts. The clue can be the sun, moon, or stars; a prevailing wind; an oriented, distant sound, such as a waterfall; a perceptible, changing elevation, general rather than local; a bearing determined by a compass or other instrument; and a variety of additional natural or instrumental clues—but never, we may be sure, an "inborn faculty of orientation." In route finding especially, man is not an island unto himself but must depend on a geographical or some other orientating relationship to find his way.

Man's so-called (unfounded) "innate sense of direction" has now been tested quite extensively. One

of many rather significant tests was made by a prairie-
state university on a day selected because there was
no wind for a possible, influencing, directional guide
—also, a heavily overcast day to avoid any guiding di-

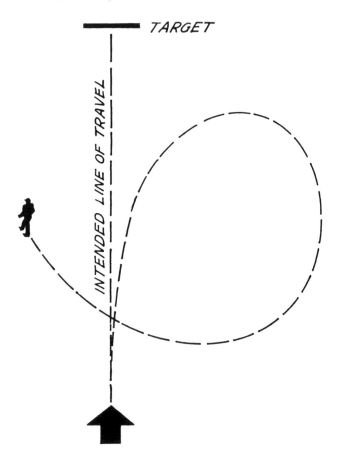

FIG. I   *Man's Tendency to Circle*

rectional heat from the sun. A large, white, cloth target was placed on the horizon. After facing the target for orientation, the participants, blindfolded and with soundproof headgear, were asked to walk what they felt was a straight line to the target. *All pursued a circuitous course.* A similar tendency to circle took place when, blindfolded, the participants were asked to drive a jeep to the target. Even when blindfolded drivers were directed over a straight line by companion passengers with open vision, drivers felt a continual, compulsive urge to pursue the circuitous course as the logical one. In subsequent tests, blindfolded operators of watercraft and those on horseback also felt this same strange compulsion to veer from the course.

Tests resulting in failure to keep a direct course often brought indignation and in some instances even violent, reactionary, and unreasoned protests from the participants. Thus, man's pet delusions and his willful thinking, we may be sure, are torn from him only with much displeasure—an important determining factor we can well afford seriously to consider in our entire route-finding program as it applies both to ourselves and to others. Since we so often discover positive and valuable information from negative results, it would seem that we might do well to suppress our fictional fancies—especially the perversity we tend to nurture about our "sense of direction"—if we are to accept the apparent, inevitable truths which apply to route finding. If we can evaluate the importance of accumulated knowledge and perception against the common "innate-directional-sense" fallacy, our route-finding program will find a much clearer horizon.

Outdoorsmen of long experience usually travel with apparent ease of orientation in familiar regions —generally unaware of actually using their long-acquired, perceptive clues, rather than what they think is a special innate sense. They are very proud of their ability, as certainly they should be. And it isn't at all strange, of course, that we find ourselves treading on rather testy ground when we question the "instinctive" or "innate" aspect of their actual perceptive ability.

Numerous theories have been advanced regarding the basic reasons why we unconsciously pursue a circuitous course. One belief is that all human beings are, in varying degrees, physically lopsided—one side of the body being heavier than the other. Another belief is that the veering is due to a measurable difference in leg length. Swimmers, for example, may have one arm stronger than the other, depending on whether they happen to be right- or left-handed, and this might seem to determine the direction toward which they veer. However, in tests, some blindfolded, right-handed swimmers have, strangely enough, circled to the left, others to the right, while left-handed swimmers also have veered in both directions.

A rather dominant theory among psychologists— and perhaps in the final analysis the most logically valid one to date—is that we have some sort of a circling mechanism in our central nervous system.

Facing rain, snow, sun, and heavy wind during travel are factors that sometimes create a tendency to veer, when, for protection, we are inclined to hold our heads less than straightforward to avoid the discomfort of these elements.

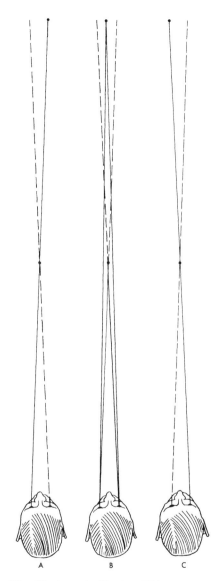

FIG. 2   *The Illusion of Aligning Objects*

One rather strange cause for our tendency to veer from a straight course—perhaps more an optical illusion than a delusion—is the mistaken concept that we can travel a straight course by an alignment of objects. While using both eyes to align distant objects, we do reasonably well. We find upon closing one eye, our dominant eye, that the objects remain in line; but as we close the other eye, the intermediate object appears to jump out of line. Try this with a pencil held before your eyes at arm's length, aligned with a distant object. Close one eye at a time and continue sighting. In most instances, one eye will throw the pencil to one side, while the other will generally permit alignment. The eye which permits alignment is the dominant eye. It is clear then that travel on any predetermined alignment course, such as from stake to stake, tree to tree, or other object to object, requires the application of our dominant or "sighting eye," whether it be the right or the left eye, if we are to avoid the strange inclination to veer.

The difference in the leg-length theory, for example, would seem to be a sound, physically obvious reason for veering; but this factor alone has proved insufficient in tests for a valid conclusion. Two individuals with longer right than left legs have on occasion in such tests veered in opposite directions. All factors in each individual's makeup, therefore, need broad, composite consideration for any comprehensive understanding of man's veering tendencies.

Perhaps it is not important in a concise book of this kind, or even in actual practice for that matter, to ponder the basic, technical reasons for veering off course. Our prime awareness, I think, should be that naturally and invariably we do veer one way or the other and are able to prevent doing so only through the aid of tangible clues, natural or instrumental. We might gain an advantage if we placed ourselves in a special category by learning whether we veer to the right or left and the actual extent of our tendency to pursue a circuitous course.

When we apply a compass or other instrument to route finding, it would seem that we could leave our delusions and willful thinking behind and rely on the technical application alone of such instruments. Yet, here, too, illusory human factors creep in to upset this instrumental advantage. The magnetic compass seems to be the most commonly misunderstood and misapplied of all route-finding instruments—presumably because it has had such wide use among both lay and professional wilderness travelers and because of the extreme magnetic variations which act upon the compass at different points on the earth.

The most common misconceptions about the magnetic compass are that the needle "points to the north," that it "points toward the magnetic pole"—or, in fact, that it necessarily *points* to anything in particular.

A small compasslike device set into the stock of a gun is often used on the theory that if the hunter on entering a wild area uses his gun barrel as a direction pointer in coincidence with this compass device, all he needs for a return routing to his starting point is to redirect the gun-barrel pointing in the opposite direction.

If he were to walk on unobstructed, level ground, continually watching the compass device, this going-

and-coming concept could possibly be valid. In actual practice, however, the user will accumulate a vast amount of side drift away from his course—so-called lateral error—in any rough country, caused by walking around obstacles particular to certain wild regions, such as swamps, ponds, lakes, bog and muskeg, swales and ravines, hills, cliffs, down timber, arroyos, gulches, mesas, and hummocks. The total errors due to these obstacles throw him widely off any possible straight return course.

The hunter's return direction in using the compass device will very roughly, it is true, parallel his line of departure; but most likely the two lines of travel—the going and the coming—will, by the side-drift deviations mentioned, have become a surprising and confusing distance apart. While this gun-compass device can be a valuable aid and a worthwhile purchase when used with sounder travel methods, the hunter should not be led to believe that the device will direct him back to his starting point. The same general departure-and-return misconception also applies in principle to the use of a regular compass, as a later chapter will endeavor to point out.

And what about the various "natural" guides to direction? These have been many and too often illusory. The oldest and most familiar is that moss always grows heaviest on the north side of a tree. The reasoning behind this certainly seems logical enough: moss is most apt to thrive where an accumulation of snow and moisture naturally remains longest, in the constantly shaded wet places of least evaporation—the side of the tree least affected by the sun's rays. Yet, upon wide examination this natural-growth factor is not consistently borne out. Moss is found growing indiscriminately on all sides of trees, due to widely varying circumstances of shade, moisture, and sunlight penetration into forest areas, thus wholly confusing the value of this purported directional theory.

Another suggested natural guide to direction finding is that a tree growing in an open area will have the heaviest branches predominantly on the sunniest side. This also seems logical enough. However, if you step outdoors and examine even isolated trees in full, unobstructed sunlight, you most likely will find predominant branch growth varying toward all sides—at least not with any apparent general predominance on the sunniest side that can be used as a reliable directional clue.

On the same sunlight-influencing-growth-predominance theory, it has been claimed that annual ring growth in the trunks of trees is heaviest on that side having the most exposure to the sun—again a seemingly logical concept, but one having no truly apparent directional significance.

One way of getting at the statistical certainties of using natural directional clues is to consider the law of probability on a hike through the country. In evaluating average natural directional clues, unless we came up with a very much higher than 50–50 average factor of such clues, their directional value would be quite worthless. In a roughly 50–50 average, one half would completely cancel out the directional value of the other half. If we cannot cut a few simple notches into trees with a camp ax and thus readily observe the directional predominance of annual ring growth or see a heavier branch growth consistently apparent on one side, these clues can have little or no practical directional use. It isn't likely that in an emergency or otherwise, we would notch a large number of trees to compute natural growth averages for a direction.

It is perhaps remotely possible that if we checked a vast number of trees and fed our total comparative observations into a computer, we might come up with a very small, obscure, normally hidden, total average predominance of moss on the least sunny side of trees, heavier branch masses, and an average of wider annual ring growth on the sunny side. But after many years of subjecting these various theories to youth groups in organized camps and to adults generally, I have found the directional value of such clues quite impractical.

A common, traditional, and romantic delusion is that Indians, Eskimos, and other ethnic groups closely associated with wilderness life have exclusive, special faculties independent of their perceptive sense for finding their way through wilderness areas. That these groups manage extraordinarily well in limited areas known to them through intimate and habitual association with directional clues in their own particular region should not be questioned. But in strange country they have their share of route-finding problems along with the rest of us. Expeditions that as common practice use guides employ native guides long familiar with a more or less local region, dismissing and hiring others successively on the same premise when travel progresses into new territory.

Early Polynesians apparently demonstrated a

marked aptitude for finding their way over land and sea by using nature as a guide. While primarily they used the stars to guide them directionally, they were also able to use as a guide and for position designation the flight extent seaward of certain land birds identified with an area; familiar, detached, vegetable matter floating in the water, driven directionally by known prevailing winds and currents; the identifying smell and taste of particular waters; cloud masses that hung in suspension over islands seen from afar, and other such natural clues. Some historians have plausibly and commendably recorded this ability and pointed out the natural means of native route finding; but as so often happens in depicting the colorful life of natives in general, special innate senses have been attributed to the Polynesians and to other ethnic groups, along with a conjecture of false natural clues, until delusion has been added to delusion.

A study of nature as a route-finding guide, even in this technical day, remains extremely valuable as a complement to modern methods and instruments; but we should not be carried away with obscure fancies, concluding that we can travel with consistent accuracy over the world's wilderness areas of land and water by natural means alone. It would be a trial-and-error process at best, with most emphasis, we might assume, on error. In any event, for either planned expeditions or orderly, individual travel, we cannot be satisfied with less than positive and precise methods, both natural and technical. And now let us get on with them.

CHAPTER TWO

Why We Get Lost

THE failure properly to relate ourselves to some known factor—natural or otherwise—as a directional guide and most often the lack of systematic travel toward or return to a predetermined base line (such as a road, railroad, river, or lakeshore) rather than a specific point (such as a Hudson Bay post, cabin, or car) are the most common reasons why we get lost, or fail to move freely and successfully over wilderness land and water.

When the hunter, for example, leaves his car on a country road and walks northerly into a game area, it is not "just common sense," as we are generally led to believe, that he should simply reverse his direction and walk southerly to get back to his car. If he does and if he has gone any appreciable distance into the hunting area, the chances are that he will find the car "gone" when he again reaches the road. The car, of course, is still where he left it, but he hasn't managed by his best efforts the logical return to the place on the road where he parked the car. And he is not likely to relate his going with his coming unless he formulates his plan of travel on a much sounder principle—methods which will be considered in later chapters.

The compass line shown in the sketch below may be regarded as the hunter's intended general northerly direction. When he took a southerly compass direc-

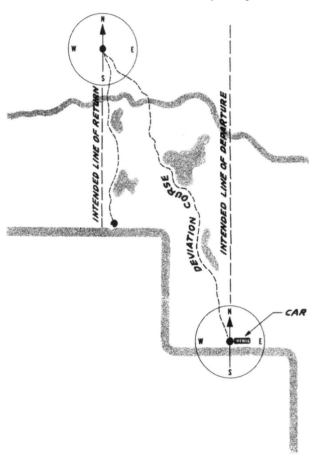

FIG. 3 *Hunter's Departure and Diverted Return*

tion for the return to his car, he reached the tote road all right, but due to side drift, he arrived at a point far removed from his car, curves in the road having concealed the car from his view.

Now the confusing question arises in his mind as to which direction on the tote road he should walk to find his car. If the road is, say, a wilderness logging or rough tote road with various side roads and Y branches of little or no current travel, he could— even though being on this man-made trail—become wholly confused and wander aimlessly into the night. There is also a chance that if he were not adjusted to wilderness travel through experience, he might even develop a twinge of panic or complete frustration, as so often happens in similar instances, when he reaches the tote road and does not immediately come upon his car. The car, he concludes, has possibly been stolen, or he speculates on the theory that haplessly he has wandered onto a strange road and not onto a segment of the tote road from which he first departed. An instance of this kind in the Midwest prompted a hunter to abandon the road and again backtrack into the woods, hoping somehow to pick up the "familiar road" from which he thought he had departed. Searchers found him days later— hungry, exhausted, and no less disillusioned.

While long-range visibility is cut off by dense growth in forest regions, curvature of the earth and terrestrial obstacles such as rolling hills and rough terrain can cut off visibility on prairie, desert, and tundra over a surprisingly limited distance of travel. Curvature of the earth seems negligible over a short distance, but few people realize the rapid increase of this curvature as the ratio of the distance multiplies. The drop in the horizon due to the earth's curvature is just slightly over a half foot the first mile, but is more than four feet in two miles. Because of the earth's curvature, a person of average height standing, say, on the shore of a lake would not even with field glasses be able to see another person of average height standing on the opposite shore six miles away on a clear day. And a horseback rider traveling over level or slightly undulating desert or prairie would, as a result of the earth's curvature, lose sight of the ranch buildings from which he departed after about ten miles.

On arctic tundra, shallow lakes are numerous, but being so much alike, they offer little individuality as distinguishable landmarks. In the summer, the necessity of bypassing these shallow lakes and ponds, the rolling tundra hills and earth's curvature, and man's tendency to circle can combine to offset a straight compass course and create the same difficult side-drift situation described for the forest traveler. The going-and-coming side-drift errors could, of course, on occasion cancel one another out, but they are also just as likely to be cumulative, and this unknown factor in itself tends to involve directional uncertainty.

Compass declination, too generally misunderstood or deliberately ignored, is responsible for a number of people getting lost. For some strange reason, compass declination (the difference at various points on the earth between where the compass needle comes directionally to magnetic rest and true north and south) is for the most part disregarded by the lay-

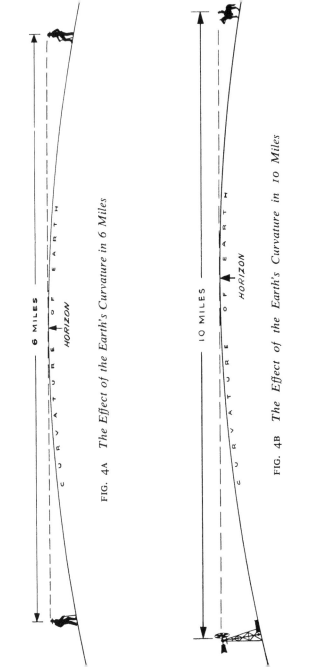

FIG. 4A   *The Effect of the Earth's Curvature in 6 Miles*

FIG. 4B   *The Effect of the Earth's Curvature in 10 Miles*

man. He sees compass declination as something too technical for his concern or treats it as though it were a negligible factor of little consequence. And so he goes on using his compass with the illusion that the needle always "points" steadfastly to the north. (See Using the Compass Without Declination, in Chapter 4.)

The compass needle's directional, magnetic position can be from true north to any extreme error, depending on where the compass happens to be. When you consider that in eastern and western Canada and the United States failure to use compass declination can throw one off a mile in a little more than three miles, is it any wonder that some people get lost even with a compass when declination is disregarded?

Each year, large sums of money are spent searching for lost people. The search cost, especially in the employment of planes, has been so great in Canada, for example, that restrictions have had to be placed on private recreational travel north of the 51st parallel unless parties can properly qualify their members to the Royal Canadian Mounted Police on route-finding knowledge and competence in general wilderness travel. A share of headline-seeking crackpots have feigned being lost or have lost themselves deliberately for publicity purposes, but the large percentage of lost wilderness travelers get lost because they have inadequate route-finding knowledge.

Few private flyers or bush pilots are able to fix their positions by navigational astronomy. Most follow radio beams, highways, railroads, water courses, mountain ranges, and other landmarks. Fortunately, most private flyers do not venture very far into unfamiliar wilderness areas. But some do so foolhardily on rare occasions, as search records over the years show. Commercial bush pilots, on the other hand, become acquainted with their own areas of flight by gradually increased familiarity with geographical features and thus have maintained a remarkably good reputation for deep-wilderness travel without much technical route-finding knowledge.

Recreational canoe trippers account for a small percentage of those who get lost, especially as a result of canoe upsets where they are thrown on their own resources to survive on foot over strange land masses that are interrupted by numerous intervening lakes and rivers.*

Prospectors have in recent years added to the grand total of those becoming lost, because in their search for mineral prospects they have been compelled to go deeper into wilderness areas generally not frequented by the average hunting, fishing, and recreational fringe element—and because too many overeager, would-be prospectors extend their mineral searches beyond the scope of their wilderness experience.

Winter recreational travel in wilderness areas by tourist and sportsman is relatively small compared to such activity in milder seasons, but this limited winter travel does account for a surprising number of people getting lost, some with fatal results. The

* For a comprehensive treatment of wilderness travel and survival, see my books *The New Way of the Wilderness* and *North American Canoe Country,* published by The Macmillan Company.

most common reason for such tragedies in winter is the belief that one can readily backtrack through snow over a return route to the point of beginning. With just an average wind and loose-blown snow, snowshoe, ski, motorized toboggan, dog-sled, and foot tracks soon drift over. The tendency to circle brings some back to their own previously made, now unrecognized tracks. If the snow is light and the tracks have partly drifted in, the tracks may appear to have been made days before by strangers. Many people, through insufficient tracking skill, cannot determine which direction such weakly defined, snow-blown tracks lead. After a while utter confusion or even panic may set in. On occasion, some people in desperation make the mistake of heading out blindly over unbroken snow in a direction they "instinctively" believe will return them to their point of beginning. In sub-zero weather, tragedy can here dog their tracks.

The mind plays strange directional tricks in the wilderness. Some of the most rational and methodical people become utterly muddled in their thinking at actually finding themselves lost.

In a particular instance, a man followed a stream for half a day, knowing full well that he was going downstream, but upon leaving the stream to avoid a steep contour along the bank and again returning to the stream, he found, because of a sharp, hairpin bend in the stream, that it appeared to be flowing in the wrong direction. The least play of the imagination at such moments of confusion may suggest to an individual in these circumstances that he has come upon another stream, or perhaps a tributary of the original stream.

Frequently, we find those who in an impulse of uneasiness about their direction confuse the ends of the compass needle. So widespread has this confusion been over the years that manufacturers have been obliged to create compasses with revolving dials or to stamp N and S on the ends of the needle for directional identification of its magnetic alignment.

It is not unusual to find those who in a moment of directional stress, adamantly refuse to accept even the reading of a properly working compass unaffected by magnetic disturbance. "It just doesn't seem to point in the right direction," they say. Many compass needles show a polarity distinction by black and clear metal. It is well beforehand to mark this directional distinction of the needle on the back of the compass box.

Extensive travel into wilderness areas is not always the main cause for people getting lost. Tourists have become seriously lost by wandering a few feet from their cabins into a forest area. A man parked his car and family on the shoulder of a Canadian highway and hurried into the forest to satisfy an urgent need. He was never seen again. Another was lost going from a cabin to a nearby woodlot for fuel. He was found days later and miles away in a pitiable condition. Blueberry pickers a few hundred yards from their cars or canoes have literally disappeared.

Little consideration has been given over the years to the educational prevention of getting lost. Undoubtedly, deeply rooted reasons for this exist. Most hunters and fishermen will not, as a rule, admit to their incompetence as outdoorsmen or to their fear of getting lost. To some others the possibility of becoming lost is not sufficiently apparent. We need to recognize as a basic postulate that wilderness-travel inability among the majority of recreational travelers is widespread and shrouded in a sort of silent desperation. The focus, unfortunately, of a large percentage of hunters and fishermen has been on big game bags and full fish creels—not generally on the acquisition and value of wilderness knowledge.

Sweden seems to have taken the lead in the route-finding field by setting up orientation programs in their elementary schools. These are excellent combinations of play, study, and physical fitness. Periodic field games of orientation are held—compass courses walked and run for competitive prizes or curricular credits. Orienteering training, as it is now called, is beginning to spill over from Sweden into Canada and to some extent into the United States, thanks to the untiring and generous effort of the chief exponent of this school promotion plan, Björn Kjellström. We might do well to emulate the thorough Swedish program in our national recreational and professional wilderness life.

CHAPTER THREE

Maps and Map Reading

Maps can be infinitely fascinating documents. On wilderness maps the blank spaces are apt to conjure up more lust for romance and adventure than the well-delineated areas. One speculates at length on what natural wonders lie within these wilderness voids. Some of the greatest explorations in history have been inspired by maps and traced at their inception before an open fire in an armchair, or by several participants of an exploration party seated around a table spread luxuriously with a virtual feast of maps.

Perhaps the most common impression gained from the word "map" are the gas-station folders which guide us over the country's highways—in themselves a tremendous feat of compilation. Maps fill a vast variety of purposes. We can even have maps showing such unusual characteristics of the earth as population growth based on some indigenous quality of the soil, mineral maps of the nation's geodetic resources, and so on into just about every field of human endeavor. We should certainly not overlook the pictorial beauty of maps and their priceless value as art treasures.

As we travel the wilderness trails of the world, we need maps which, of course, primarily concern route finding. But they must also be slanted to fit the specific nature or purpose of our wilderness travel and no less comply with the form of transportation we shall use. There is a great deal of difference, for example, between a map designed for packhorse trails and one adapted to canoe routes.

I hasten at the start to point out these various obvious factors since maps are too often regarded as mere prosaic geographical sheets of paper featuring an area of the earth.

When early cartographers attempted to lay out the surface areas of the spherical world on a flat sheet, they became involved in a rather complicated and baffling process. Apparently it is impossible to flatten such surfaces without their original curvature patterns suffering some distortion. A number of ingenious dodges were attempted to avoid the distortion, but none of the final results was really successful. We have, however, managed quite well to tolerate consequent errors by applying a system of survey corrections when the land and water patterns deviate too badly from place to place. For all practical purposes in our wilderness route finding we can disregard the errors incurred by this flat representation of the earth's curvature since it could affect us only if we became involved in a special process of technical exploration mapping, a subject beyond the immediate scope or need of this book.

The most essential map requirement early in a country's development was to provide a grid of some kind that would permit designating particular points

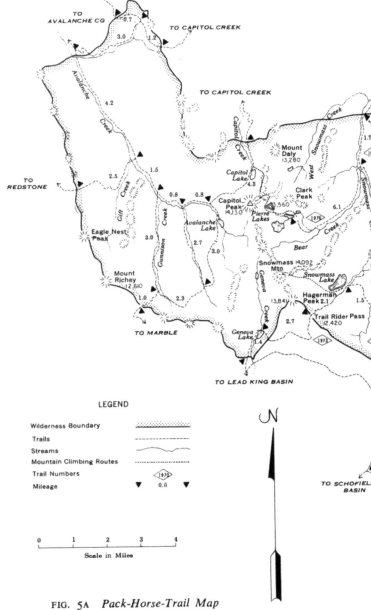

FIG. 5A *Pack-Horse-Trail Map*

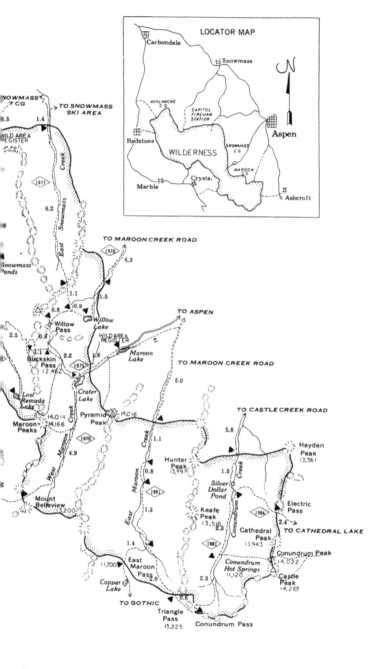

LOCATOR MAP

Carbondale

Snowmass

AVALANCHE CG

CAPITOL FIREMAN STATION

Redstone

WILDERNESS

SNOWMASS CG

Aspen

MAROON CG

Marble

Crystal

Ashcroft

CN

SNOWMASS CG

.5   1.4

TO SNOWMASS SKI AREA

WILD AREA REGISTER

1977

6.2

East Snowmass Creek

Snowmass Ponds

TO MAROON CREEK ROAD

1978

6.3

1.1   1.5

0.8   0.9

Willow Pass

Willow Lake

WILD AREA REGISTER

TO ASPEN

2.5   0.8

Maroon Lake

TO MAROON CREEK ROAD

1.1   2.2

Buckskin Pass 12,462

1975   1.6

5.0

Lost Remuda Lake

Crater Lake

14,014   14,018

Maroon Peaks   14,166

Pyramid Peak

TO CASTLE CREEK ROAD

1970

5.8

4.9

Hayden Peak 13,561

West Maroon Creek

East Maroon Creek

1.1

Hunter Peak 13,497

0.8

1.5

Silver Dollar Pond

Conundrum Creek

Electric Pass

1981

1984

Mount Bellview 12,000

1.3

Keefe Peak 13,516

Cathedral Peak 13,943

2.4

TO CATHEDRAL LAKE

2.3

1981

Conundrum Peak 14,022

1.4

11,700

East Maroon Pass

2.0

Conundrum Hot Springs 11,120

Castle Peak 14,265

Copper Lake

2.3

TO GOTHIC

0.6

Triangle Pass 13,225

Conundrum Pass

on the earth surface and also allow an orderly and systematic method for describing land and water areas for various uses. With this land-demarkation system fairly well accomplished, the amenities and attributes of modern mapping naturally followed.

We get a fairly good picture in our mind's eye of how the world's surface has been laid out and mapped for identifying such points and land areas if instead of confining our point of view to a flat map alone we first take a broad objective view of the whole earth sphere. A peeled orange suggests rather graphically on its surface design one kind of earth division, because the lines indicating the orange segments are similar to the longitude lines of the earth from pole to pole. The orange I peeled a moment ago had about a dozen or more segments. The longitude lines of the earth, on the other hand, have been divided into 360 surface segments, called degrees. These individual degrees can be divided into 60 parts, which are called minutes of arc. A minute of arc, in turn, can be divided into 60 more parts, called seconds of arc. If in your bent for precision you are not happy to stop there, you can do what the geodetic survey does: divide the seconds of arc into hundredths of seconds of arc.

Other chapters give special emphasis to lines of position. If you are of a mind to call the longitudinal lines in this chapter lines of position, it is perfectly proper to do so. For the purpose of designating your position, you can, as indicated in other chapters, say that wherever you are on the earth's surface, you will inevitably be on one of these longitudinal position lines.

FIG. 5B *Canoe-Route Map*

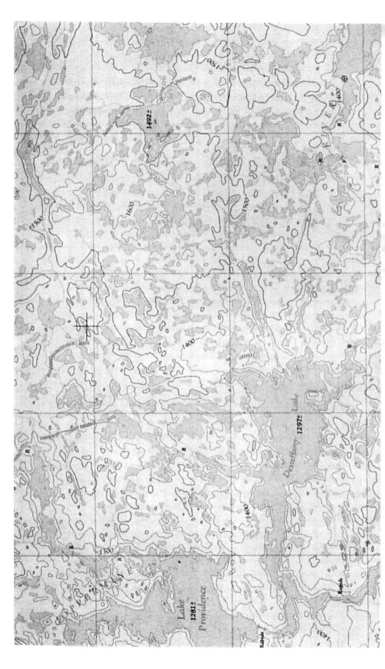

If we run a series of lines around the world that cross the longitude lines, we get the earth surface divided into squarish portions. Whereas the longitude lines come to a point at the poles, like the segment lines of an orange, the latitude lines parallel one another. Yet here again we divide the earth surface into degrees, called latitude; divide the degrees into 60 parts, called minutes; and in turn divide the minutes into 60 parts, called seconds, and so on.

Thus, we come up with longitude lines running from pole to pole and latitude lines running around

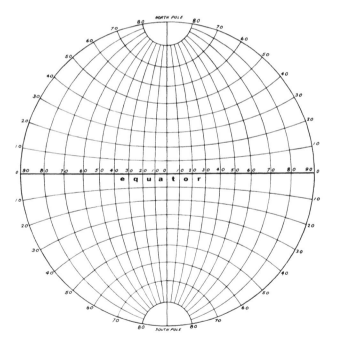

FIG. 6   *Earth Sphere Showing Latitude and Longitude*

the earth to intersect, or cross, the longitude lines, as shown in the illustration.

We can now easily point out a position anywhere on the earth surface by two numbers: one of longitude, the other of latitude. One might assume that the numbers for each would go from 0 to 360, but this is not the case. Rather, the longitude lines were started at Greenwich, England, where the longitude is 0. Then the longitude was numbered east to 180 degrees and west to 180 degrees. This really amounts to the same thing as going from 0 to 360, except that we have to use the term east or west longitude and go only to 180 degrees in either direction from Greenwich. In numbering latitude lines, the equator becomes 0 and the numbering goes up only to 90 in both north and south directions, ending with the 90 figure at the poles. Therefore, we say north or south latitude as the case may be, meaning a particular latitude line situated north or south of the equator.

Therefore, say that we described a point as 56 degrees north latitude and 117 degrees west longitude. This would put us on a point somewhere near the Peace River in Alberta, Canada. For greater accuracy of our position, we would have it read something like this: 56 degrees, 12 minutes, 14 seconds north latitude; and 117 degrees, 10 minutes, 04 seconds west longitude. If we wanted to go into decimals too, we could pinpoint a very precise spot.

Where we have a sheet map (a portion of the earth surface, or even all of the earth surface, laid out by projection on a flat plane), we can do the same thing, that is, use two numbers to designate a point. Along the side margins of the map we have the latitude numbers laid out for us; along the top and bottom,

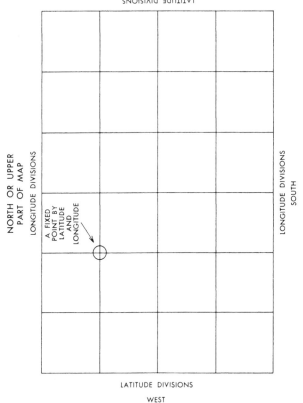

FIG. 7   *Flat Map Segment of Earth Surface Using Two*
Numbers (Latitude and Longitude) to Fix a
Point

the longitude numbers. Therefore, it becomes a
simple matter to run a finger or a straightedge out
to the margins of the map from a particular point we
select and read off the latitude and longitude of our
position. Or, inversely, we can use longitude and

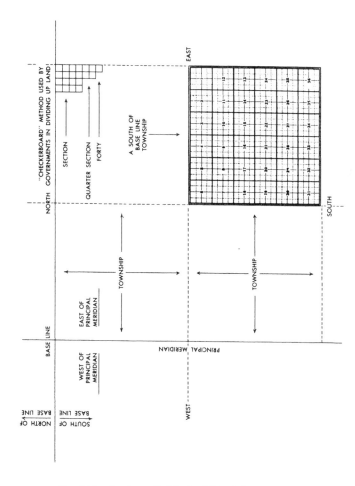

FIG. 8 *"Checkerboard" Method Used by Governments in Dividing Up Land*

latitude numbers and move in from the top and
side margins of the map to find a particular geographical point (see Fig. 7).

With this information and adequate wilderness-
travel knowledge, we should be able to find a point
on the Peace River, or anywhere, as accurately as a
street number in a certain city, state, and country.

We could also designate a position somewhere by
the "checkerboard" method used by governments
in dividing up land. The plan is quite easy to follow.
When a region is still in its undeveloped state, two
long lines are laid out by survey in a particular wilderness area, one running north and south, called a
meridian; the other east and west, called a base line.
(Some meridian and base lines extend over many
miles and have become rather famous both geographically and historically. Some have even been
given celebrity names in addition to their numbers.)
As will readily be seen, this vertical and horizontal
survey gets us right back to the basic principle of
having a line of position intersect a base line. These
parent meridian and base lines form the starting
points or lines of position from which land is divided
for settlement east and west, north and south. First, a
square 6 miles by 6 miles is set up, making 36
square miles, or what is called a township. The
accompanying illustration "Section Location" em-
phasizes the position of the section relative to others
in the same township and to those in adjoining townships. These relative positions also become important
in designating one's position when traveling from
section to section and township to township. (A row
of these townships is called a range.) Each one of
the 36 square miles is called a section of land and

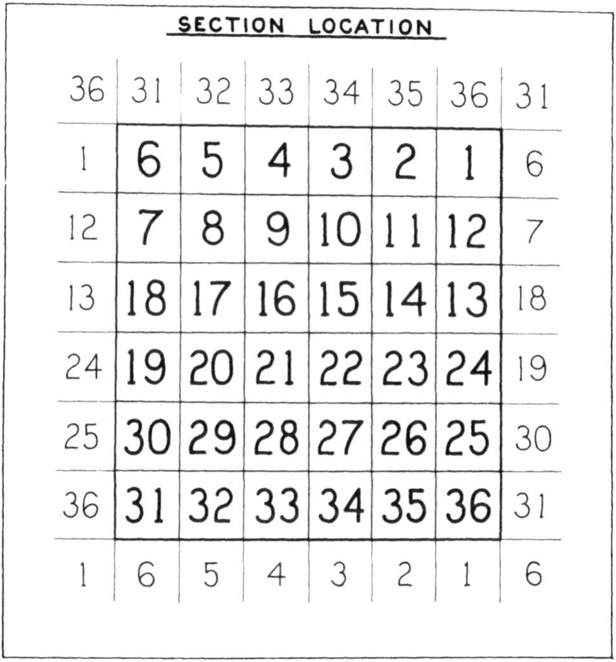

SECTION LOCATION

36	31	32	33	34	35	36	31
1	6	5	4	3	2	1	6
12	7	8	9	10	11	12	7
13	18	17	16	15	14	13	18
24	19	20	21	22	23	24	19
25	30	29	28	27	26	25	30
36	31	32	33	34	35	36	31
1	6	5	4	3	2	1	6

FIG. 9A   *Section Location*

contains 640 acres. The checkerboard system continues; each square mile or section divided into 4 parts, called quarter sections; each quarter section contains 160 acres. (Incidentally, most homesteads in the early days contained a quarter section.) Quarter sections are divided up into 4 parts called forties, or 40 acres. Where there are water areas that might leave irregular fragments of forties along a shore or as islands, the fragments are then given a further subdivision called government lots.

We can readily designate our position on a map or delineate a parcel of land by this checkerboard

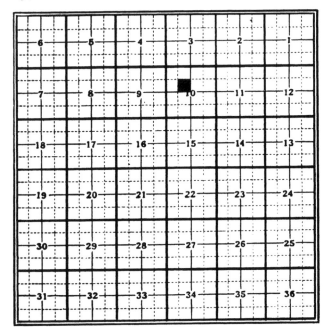

FIG. 9B   *A Blocked Out Forty to Show Its Location in
Section 10*

system. Say we wish to indicate the position of our
government lot number 6, on which we have a water-
front cabin. Our description then, picking arbitrary
numbers for our example, would read: "Government Lot 6, in the Northwest Quarter of Section 10,
Township 32 North, Range 19 West, east of the
4th Principal Meridian." If we had a full 40 acres
in a square, our description would run something like
this: "The Southeast Quarter of the Northwest
Quarter of Section 10, Township 32 North, Range

19 West, east of the 4th Principal Meridian" (see Fig. 9B). If we wanted to designate an exact point of position, we could use the above description and just begin with "The Northeast Corner of the Southeast Quarter . . ."

Sometimes land areas are subdivided by individual survey and platted into various-size tracts for residential lots, mining claims, or other special purposes, and the plats are placed on file as a permanent record in the office of the county registrar or county clerk. We would then give the description of an area or point something like this: "Lot 5 in Fair Oaks Subdivision, Section 8, Township 14 North, Range 19 West, east of the 4th Principal Meridian." In designating an exact point or position we would say, for example: "A point situated on the west line of Lot 5, which point is 37 feet south from the Northwest Corner of said lot," and then continuing as in the above description.

Wilderness maps often are given other "checkerboard" divisions based on an entirely different plan from that of the foregoing. The checkerboard squares on some canoe maps in Canada, for example, are laid down on a scale of 1 inch to 4 miles. In other words, the map is divided into 1-inch squares, each square representing an area 4 miles by 4 miles. The maps could be made on a scale of 2 miles to an inch or 8 miles to an inch, which sometimes they are. Or they could be laid out on a 10,000 meter grid (roughly 6.2 miles). But the general checkerboard principle of division is basically the same. The legend of the map will then show that an inch on the map equals a certain number of miles on the actual ground.

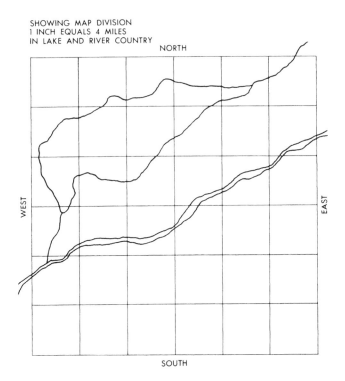

SHOWING MAP DIVISION
1 INCH EQUALS 4 MILES
IN LAKE AND RIVER COUNTRY

FIG. 10   *Map Division Showing Scale 1 Inch to 4 Miles*

Most maps are made on what we call a graphic scale. Generally, there is no checkerboard division of the area in this instance as in the preceding systems, simply a scale—a unit of measurement such as that shown in Figure 11. This system, while not as convenient as some others, is very good because

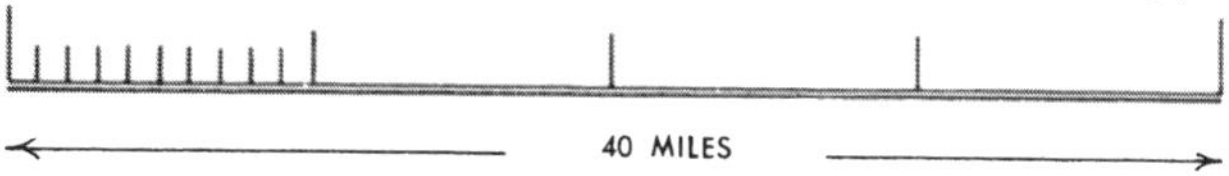

FIG. 11 *Graphic Scale of Miles*

enlargement or reduction of the map does not change the scale relative to the map itself. When you use the graphic scale, it makes no difference in which direction you lay out your wilderness route. The scale can be used to measure off the miles by laying a ruler, a straw, or just a slip of paper along the scale and applying that measurement, in multiples if necessary, to the total distance to be measured on the map.

The numeral or fraction-scale system is used on most maps in conjunction with other measuring systems. It simply shows the relative size of the map area as compared to the actual land and water area, often on a basis of one to one million, written 1:1,000,000. This means that 1 inch on the map represents 1,000,000 inches on the ground or water. Converted for convenience of measurement, 1,000,000 inches roughly equal 16 miles plus. Thus, 1 inch on the map represents about 16 miles on land or water. Of course, any ratio can be used, such as one to ten thousand, one to a hundred million, and so forth.

One difficulty encountered by cartographers is a satisfactory way of portraying elevations such as hills, mesas, slopes, mountains, etc., on the flat surface of a map. The problem is that on the map these elevations must be shown as viewed from above the elevation, whereas our conception of them, unless we are flying, is to see them from a point more or

FIGS. 12A, B   *Elevations by Contour Lines and Shading*

less to one side. All sorts of experimental drawing
methods have been used to show such relief, in-
cluding hatching, shading, and contour lines. While
none of these gives a wholly realistic impression of
elevations, we do, nevertheless, become familiar with
the shortcomings of such drawings and accept an
arbitrary pattern of contour lines and shading which
helps us to visualize hills and mountains.

Before the advent of aerial mapping, the task of
map making was enormous. Areas had to be surveyed and every detail laboriously drawn in. Yet,
some extraordinary accomplishments in map making by early explorers have been handed down.
Now, the earth surface is charted by a series of
photographs from the air, the cartographer's remain-
ing job being to fit these numerous "jigsaw" photo-
graphic pieces into a vast map pattern. The cartographer then designates the elevations and brings in

all other information needed—still an undertaking of no small proportion despite the advantage of aerial photography.

The particular purpose and nature of an expedition or journey, as indicated earlier, will, of course, determine the map selection. On a canoe map, bodies of water will be clearly delineated, and the length and location of portages will be shown. Also indicated will be rapids and falls with drop in feet; marsh, bog, and open muskeg; woods, tundra and prairie; height in feet of various water levels above the sea; district boundaries; trading posts; names of lakes and rivers when they have names (many are unnamed); direction of water flow; compass declination; latitude and longitude scales along the margins, and such other general information as will be pertinent to the particular canoe country.

Thus we see how the above canoe maps of the Pre-Cambrian Shield of the northern United States and Canada differ from maps of the Southwest wilderness or other somewhat similar regions of the world where travel is by pack horse, camel, foot, or possibly jeep. Elevations in such areas take on a special significance for indicating roughness of country, with the chief emphasis on the kinds of trails, water holes, oases, available grazing areas, refueling stations, and other essentials pertinent to travel overland.

Maps in their most elementary form can be merely a few lines scratched in the sand with a stick, a page from a notebook on which a few pencil scrawls have been drawn, a priceless piece of sketched parchment made centuries ago; or a map can be what it is today, a highly developed, lithographed sheet produced by modern cartographers and civil engineers. Perhaps there is no pat formula for defining the word "map." Derived from the Latin word *"mappa,"* meaning napkin, its origin does not convey much as a description. A map could be called a symbolized segment of earth drawn to scale on a horizontal projection or, more simply, a chart of land. Perhaps one should refer to a map as a miniaturization of a segment, or all, of the earth's surface features expressed on a flat plane. Whatever the description, we need to remember that maps hold an exalted place in history, art, adventure, literature, romance, and modern-day exploration. So let us treasure our maps well and read them profoundly when we can.

The phrase "map reading" reminds me of the language problem I have with the Southwestern, Spanish-speaking people who live near a ranch I purchased on the Pecos River of New Mexico. My few Spanish words are understood by them all right, but I do not understand the answers these words elicit. So it is with maps. It is one thing to read the maps themselves, another to address them to the elements of nature and come up with significant answers.

Relating the map to the terrain might more easily be done at 20,000 feet above the particular area produced on the map. Using the map at ground level in the wilderness means not only that the map must be read from a poor vantage point, but also that the elements of nature, in their surface-view distortion, must be fully equated with the map itself.

The preceding material in this chapter will, I

think, indicate that most people could read the documentary aspects of a map with a little study, but having accomplished this initial phase, *how do you read the earth?* And how do you relate the earth factors to the map factors? The general failure to complete this relationship has been one of the major problems in route finding. It is analogous to relating an academic education to the problems of real life.

The difficulty entailed in joining map and natural terrain is that little of the apparent, natural scene corresponds with the map. Distant islands, for example, do not appear insular. They seem to be fused to the mainland or they drop from view behind the horizon due to the earth's curvature. Prominent points of land do not stand out in contrast against the water as points. Meandering, irregular bodies of water seem to terminate nearer than their far shores would indicate. Water areas tend not to assume the same shape suggested by the map, because you do not see them from above but from an angle of deceptive perspective. Mountains appear much closer than they actually are, even when unaffected by the illusion of a mirage. The intervening land areas or lakes in front of the mountain range lose their significant and identifying factors due to both perspective distortion and earth curvature. Mountains may seem low or nonexistent because of the earth's curvature. A rim on a coulee or canyon may deceptively turn out to be a mesa, or a mesa turn out to be a rim. The list of such illusions could go on indefinitely, but you get the point.

I could now, of course, use the standard dodge by saying that map reading requires experience and that in time you will acquire the knack. But you did not buy this book to read evasive abstractions.

If what is contained in other chapters of this volume is digested, you should be well along the road toward equating maps with wilderness areas. None of us, I must add, can match natural factors with map factors when the natural factors are invisible behind horizons. It is well to leave them obscured both in thought and vision until they loom into view for inspection as route-finding clues. Careful examination of nearby clues reveals a lot more than vague anticipation of distant ones.

If with a map we become uncertain about our position, the best advice seems to be: STOP. Get out the compass and start taking compass bearings to analyze the natural pattern. That bay on the right, for example, according to the map, should be a little east of north from our own position. The map also indicates that the bay is about a quarter mile deep. Let's check it. According to the map we should have an open view along a particular compass bearing about 5 miles down the lake from this point—a good identifying clue. A little practice will tell us whether a distant shore is 10, 5, or 2 miles away, although optical illusion may play tricks here. That shore off to the right as charted on the map should run approximately northeast and southwest—another important clue determined by compass bearing. Moreover, we came out of an area that can be checked for relative clues and also serve to fix our position. We passed some narrows about a mile apart. That should put us about where we are with an hour's paddling, and so forth.

In the mountains, desert, prairie, and barrens, we apply the same general logic to every natural factor in the area, not forgetting the importance of triangulation and clues to position given at length in other chapters.

The plan becomes apparent. A combination of natural, identifiable factors is not, by the law of averages, apt to occur in the same number, kind, and nature as stated in the examples above except in one place, so that by careful deduction, using these several natural factors, our position on the map can pretty well be determined. *This job of equating map and natural factors is the only map reading that can have any practical, functional value where route finding is concerned.*

If we try not to be misguided by the various optical illusions which distances, perspective, earth curvature, fog, rain, snow, mirage, and dust storms set up and if we take each natural factor into consideration as it is made available visually for identification along the trail, the road ahead should not become vague or misleading, and maps will not be the puzzles which they so often seem to be. The best possible all-around practice in relating a map to a natural environment is to determine (whenever opportunity and study allow) how many natural factors in the terrain one actually can identify with the map.

Field study by competent map-reading students has shown that the actual number of such identifying factors will far exceed our expectation. Even the layman with his wits about him can reveal enough comparable factors between map and terrain to travel the wilderness routes of the world. And with sustained practice he eventually begins to move with that unfolding vision of a veteran.

CHAPTER FOUR

The Compass

Historians have not been able to determine conclusively who invented the magnetic compass or where it originated—an early indication that it first appeared in China, or even one of several western Asiatic countries, now is obscured in a nebula of uncertainty. Perhaps the origin of the compass should be regarded more as a discovery than an invention. Loadstone, a mineral possessing magnetic qualities of polarity (magnetite), was discovered an estimated 2,000 or more years ago.

All that was required to make loadstone into a crude though effective compass was to suspend the loadstone in such a way that it would swing into its magnetic-seeking directional position. In the earliest stages this was accomplished by bonding loadstone to cork or other buoyant material and setting it in water so that it would float around into its magnetic-seeking position. When a loadstone bar or "needle" was eventually mounted so as to rotate on a pivot, its progress to the modern, jeweled, calibrated compass became largely a matter of routine refinement.

This refinement ran through a long historical de-

FIG. 13   *Bowl with Loadstone*

velopment of various compass types—the greatest problems involving suitable adaptations to seagoing vessels and aircraft. Every manner of compass appeared over the years, from the simplest type to binnacled magnetic compasses filled with fluid for damping the needle, and on to the nonmagnetic, polaroid, astro and gyro developments. In this book we shall be concerned only with highly portable units for wilderness travel.

A magnetic compass basically then is a direction-indicating instrument having a bar or needle of magnetized metal with a positive and a negative pole balanced on a delicate pivot, usually a semi-precious jewel, mounted for portable convenience in a protective, nonmagnetic box or case where the needle can rotate around a 360-degree dial or a dial of cardinal points and come to rest directionally according to the variable attractions of the earth's magnetic field.

The simplest type of magnetic compass is supplied with a rotating needle on a pivot and a stationary

FIG. 14A *Wrist Strap Compass*

dial, having only the four cardinal points: North, South, East, and West, usually initialed N, S, E, W. Such compasses are intended to give only rough general directions and often are mounted with an open-face dial either on a wrist strap or are pinned to a clothing lapel for continual, ready observation. Other compasses, as they become more sophisticated, have decorative dials called a rose, and include both cardinal and intercardinal points, such as Northeast (NE), North-Northeast (NNE), Southwest (SW), West-Southwest (WSW), and so forth. Still others include not only the cardinal and intercardinal points, but degree calibrations from 0 to 360. Most so-called sportsman's compasses have the degrees calibrated clockwise. Various other calibration systems are in use for military, surveying, and cruising purposes. But for our purposes in this book, the sportsman's and cruiser's (or forester's) types of compass will be considered, with special emphasis on the latter, because it has an extremely valuable calibration principle and is an ideal compass for both lay and professional use.

FIG. 14B   *Lapel Compass*

A first, inexperienced glance at a cruiser's compass might give the impression that a mistake has been made in the conventional calibration. Instead of the 0-to-360-degree-clockwise calibration of the sportsman's compass, the cruiser's type is calibrated

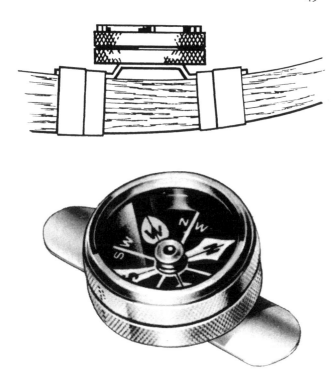

FIG. 14C *Sled, Snowshoe, and Canoe Mount Compass*

counterclockwise from 0 to 360. In addition to the counterclockwise calibration, the cardinal points have also undergone some change. North and south readings remain in their usual place on the dial face, but east and west readings have been reversed, or, as they say, transposed. The reason for this reversed or transposed order of east and west will be explained

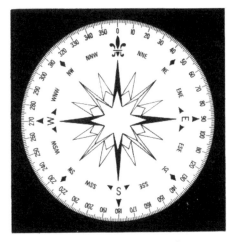

FIG. 15   *Compass Rose with Cardinal Points and Degrees*

at length later in this chapter. Also, see Quadrant
Calibration of the Compass in the Appendix,
pages 197-199.

When we examine a cruiser's compass, we find
across the inside middle of the cover a grooved white
line called a lubber's line. It is along this line that
we sight the desired compass direction. (Other
compass styles have a variety of sighting devices that
serve the same purpose as the lubber's line. Some
compasses even have elaborate telescopes with cross
hairs for accurate sighting, as we shall see later in
the description of the transit.)

On the needle of the cruiser's compass, and some
others, is a fine brass-wire-wrapping counterbalance
which can be slipped along the needle to assure horizontal balance of the needle on its delicate pivot.

This wire has not, by the way, been placed there, as we sometimes hear, to compensate for any defective manufacturing imbalance in the needle structure. If we traveled, say, only along the equatorial belt we would not have to be concerned about needle balance, because once the needle was balanced at the factory for that belt, it would remain so. In fact, the balancing wire would not be needed at all. But as we traveled any appreciable distance north or south from the equator, one end of the needle would begin to dip until it sagged off level, due to a dip attraction in the earth's magnetic field. Finally, as the travel distance increased toward either magnetic pole, the dip would be so great that one or the other end of the needle would drag inoperatively on the dial. If we continued our travel into the immediate North or South Magnetic Pole areas, the needle dip would be so extreme at one end or the other, depending on which pole we neared, that the actual position of the needle would be perpendicular.

You will recall that the compass needle cannot logically point to anything in particular. If we continue to bear this in mind, an understanding of the so-called compass "pointings" becomes much clearer. The actions of a compass needle are best described by considering that the earth is an enormous, unstable magnet, having a North Magnetic Pole at approximately 75 degrees north latitude, and 101 degrees west longitude; and a South Magnetic Pole at approximately 67 degrees south latitude, and 142 degrees east longitude. These magnetic poles must not be confused with the true North and South Poles of the earth's rotation; magnetic and earth poles are geographically far apart.

Open-Face, Cardinal Points,
0-to-360-Degree Calibration.

Cardinal and Intercardinal Points,
and 0-to-360-Degree Calibration.

FIGS. 16A, B, C *Three Types of Sportsman's Pocket
Compasses with Various Calibrations*

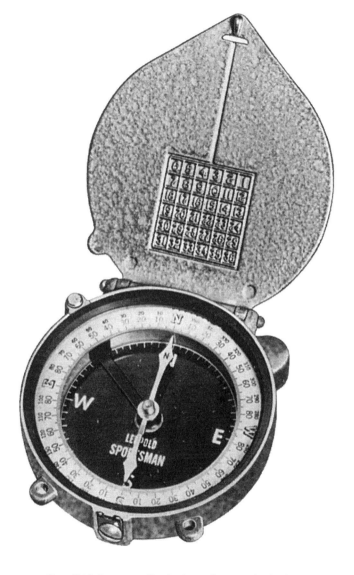

0-to-360-Degree Clockwise, Counterclockwise, and Quadrant Calibrations. Numbers on Cover Show Township Sections.

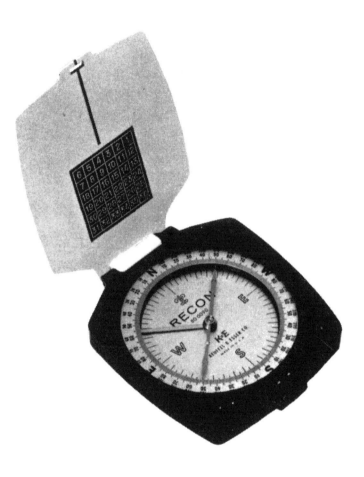

FIGS. 16D, E   *Two Types of Cruiser's (or Forester's)*
Compasses with Various Calibrations

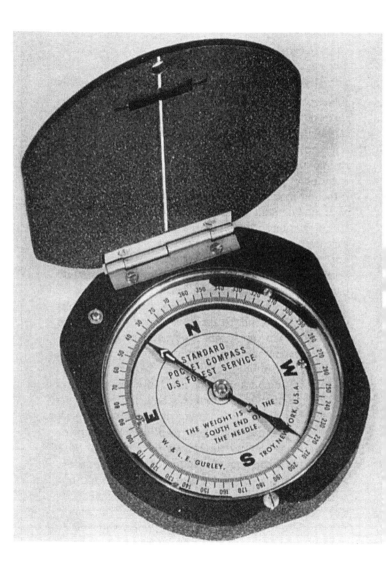

If the reader will now examine the accompanying chart showing compass declination over the earth, he will see that the actual magnetic-pole areas cover approximately 50 miles in their rough diameters—not, as most often presumed, fixed magnetic points of attraction. The chart of the earth's magnetic field shows a series of meandering magnetic lines running from one magnetic pole area to the other, each line bearing a particular identifying number.

One of these magnetic lines is called the *agonic line,* and is marked O. If the reader were anywhere on this agonic line, the direction of his compass needle would bear true north and south—the compass declination then being O.

But only directly on the agonic line does this true north-and-south pointing apply. East and west of this O, or agonic, line are other lines on the chart marked 10 degrees apart, called *isogonic lines.* Any area of the earth where these isogonic lines run, the compass needle will *not* seek a true north and south position; the needle will vary away from true north and south not in the direction of the lines but only to the degree of declination in the various areas that the isogonic-line numbers indicate (see Figs. 17A and 17B).

Areas between agonic and isogonic lines can be averaged for compass declination, but these averages, not always being consistent, must be considered only rough averages—close enough, however, for most general travel.

It is evident, then, that in no sense can we consider the needle pointing to anything. Instead of the compass needle pointing to anything in particular, it is merely seeking an alignment position at various places with the earth's magnetic field. The compass needle must not be considered to parallel the zigzag isogonic lines—a conclusion jumped to by one reader in observing a government declination chart. Isogonic lines simply indicate the particular degree of compass declination in that area where the lines run.

For convenience, that end of the needle which is commonly but incorrectly referred to as pointing to the north will be referred to as compass north or magnetic north.

The difference between true north and the direction held by the compass needle at any place is called compass declination or variation. In short, the needle declines or varies east or west from true north except on the agonic line.

We can, therefore, apply the following simple rule for setting off compass declination. *When we are west of the agonic line, the compass-north end of the needle comes to rest in a direction east of true north. When we are east of the agonic line, the compass-north end of the needle comes to rest in a direction west of true north.*

In the first instance above, the "north" end of the compass needle declines or strays east of true north; in the second, west of true north. The numbered isogonic lines show how far east or west of true north the needle declines or strays.

Up-to-date maps of the area to be traveled can be acquired from most government surveying offices. Maps can be had that show the compass declination in detail anywhere along the entire route of travel. "Up-to-date" is indicated here because compass declination changes with time, as well as place, though not uniformly or consistently. Compass declination should be checked at intervals during travel over sub-

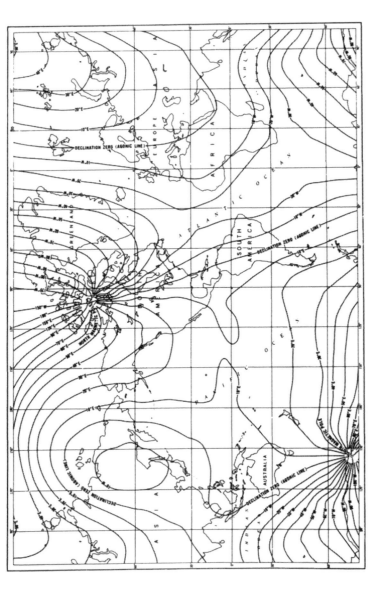

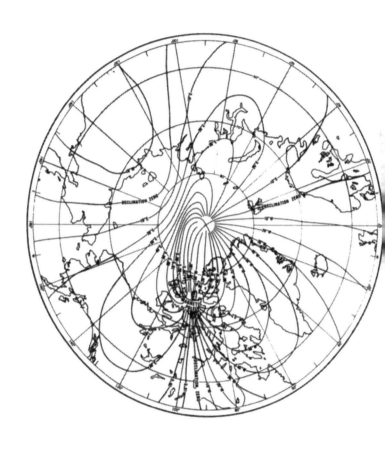

FIGS. 17A, B *Compass Declination Showing Agonic and Isogonic Lines*

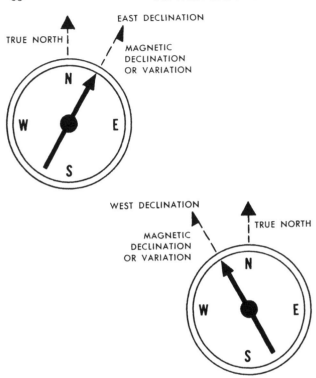

FIG. 18   *East and West Declination*

stantial wilderness areas because declination sometimes changes abruptly from place to place, and in rather strange patterns. Note, for example, the extreme irregularity of the earth's magnetic lines of force as shown in the illustrations.

If determining compass declination tends to cause the reader any difficulty, there are simple manual ways to find declination, such as the following.

Drive two slender sticks loosely into the ground—one longer than the other—and sharpen the tops to points with a knife. Sight from the point of the shorter stick to the point of the longer stick, and adjust them in the loose dirt until the points of the sticks line up with the Pole Star (Polaris, or North Star), and remember what was said in Chapter 1 about using your dominant sighting eye. With a flash-

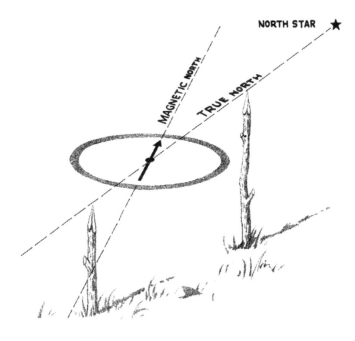

FIG. 19 *Obtaining Compass Declination by 2 Pointed Sticks*

light to illuminate the sticks and compass, you can compare true north as shown by your stick points, with compass north in degrees as shown by the compass and make the allowance for declination as you proceed on your journey the next day. Compass declination should, thus, be checked from the map or by an observation on the Pole Star every night—oftener for more positive travel.

Because the North Star does not remain in a true north position at all times, comparison of compass-needle direction with true north should be made when the star Alkaid, the trailing star at the end of the Big Dipper's handle, is in one or the other of two positions, above or below the Pole Star, as shown in Figure 20. At other positions of Alkaid, the Pole Star is slightly off true north, but at most only about 1 degree at its extreme departure from true north.

Compasses have various devices for sighting on distant objective points. Some are provided with a small half lens which allows both reading the compass face itself and viewing the distant objective point above the half lens at the same time—a split-vision principle.

Other compasses have a rotating dial. This is no more than an assembly where one or more magnetic needles or bars are attached to the underside of the dial in such fashion as to rotate the dial on a central pivot. Whatever compass type is used, the first consideration after deciding on your exact direction of travel is to apply the declination between true north and the direction held by the compass needle, then to follow the adjusted compass bearing toward your distant destination point.

FIG. 20   *Polaris for True Bearing by Position of Big Dipper*

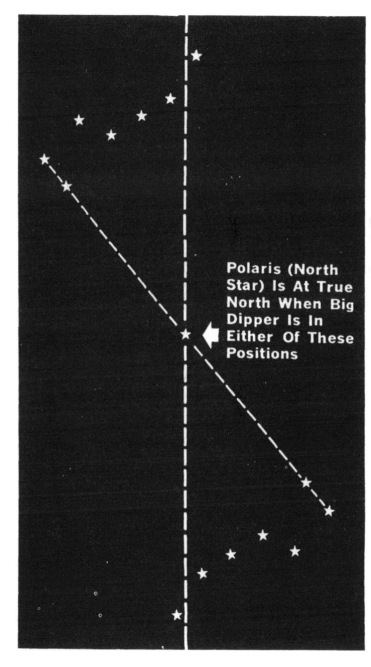
Polaris (North Star) Is At True North When Big Dipper Is In Either Of These Positions

THE CRUISER'S, OR FORESTER'S, COMPASS

In selecting a compass, the reader should give earnest consideration to acquiring the cruiser's, or forester's, type suggested earlier in this chapter. The real advantage is in its remarkable facility for sighting a course. Suppose, for example, that we wish to travel southeast. The compass is rotated in one's hand until the "north" end of the needle comes to rest over the point on the dial marked southeast. The lubber's line (sighting line on the compass cover) will then be pointing to compass southeast—not *true* southeast. For *true* southeast, allowance must be made for compass declination by swinging the compass in one's hands the required number of degrees to the right or left, whichever the east or west declination from true north happens to be. The lubber's or sighting line on the compass cover will then be pointing to *true* southeast.

Another advantage of the cruiser's, or forester's, compass—because of its more practical size and calibration from 0 to 360 degrees—is that sighting can be made on each individual degree. Instead of using only the cardinal and intercardinal points on the compass dial, such as West, Southwest, and so forth, the more precise method is to use one of the 360 calibrated degrees for a particular direction. Any of the calibrations from 0 to 360 degrees would thus provide a particular bearing or direction and be reckoned by degree number alone. This 0-to-360-degree method gives greater accuracy of bearings and is a much easier one to use for setting off the compass declination.

APPLIED PRACTICAL METHODS FOR
SETTING OFF DECLINATION

Say that we wish to travel due east. Open the cruiser's, or forester's, compass and hold it in the hands at waist level or place it on some support, away from any local magnetic disturbance such as guns and outboard motors. Be certain also that your belt buckle is brass or other nonmagnetic metal that will not attract the compass needle. Turn the compass until the "north" end of the needle rests on E (East). If after looking at the map for declination at our location, we found that true north was 20 degrees east of compass north, we would turn to the right or east until we gained 20 additional degrees. Our compass lubber's line or sight would then be pointing *true* east.

If we used the same example for finding east and applied it to one of the 360 degrees of a cruiser's, or forester's, compass instead of a cardinal point, we would turn the compass until the "north" end of the needle rested on 90 degrees, which is the same as compass east. If true north then was 20 degrees east of compass north, we would turn to the right or east until we had added 20 degrees, or 110 degrees in all. The compass lubber's line or sight would then be pointing *true* east.

Again, in another example, if we wish to travel due east, and true north in this instance happened to be 20 degrees west of compass north, we would turn the compass to the left, or west, 20 degrees. Our lubber's line would then, as before, still be pointing *true* east. (Carefully observe the compass-declination rule given earlier in this chapter.)

The foregoing examples apply to the cruiser's, or forester's, type compass having the counterclockwise calibration—*not to the sportsman's type* having the conventional dial only. Some more recent sportsman's compasses do, however, have the cruiser's type of calibration added.

A Swedish manufacturer with a service division in the United States has developed a compass for sportsmen and for the orienteering programs mentioned in Chapter 2 which has a calibrated collar for setting off declination. The aluminum needle housing is filled with liquid for damping the needle, to give rather quick readings. The compass is mounted on a rectangular, transparent base which is a valuable aid in orienting a map. A mirror in the cover with a lubber's line allows reading the degrees and sighting the distant point at the same time. The mirror also permits a back sight; that is, a sighted point behind can be made to align with a point ahead. Inches and millimeters are calibrated along the plastic base and are handy aids in making measurements on a map.

For using an ordinary sportsman's compass having a needle and fixed dial, without the cruiser's calibration, hold the compass at waist level and turn it until the compass north end of the needle comes to rest over N on the dial. If we wish to travel east and found from the declination chart that true north was 20 degrees east of where the compass north end of the needle comes to rest, we would turn to the right, or east, 20 degrees. Now, all of the readings on the compass dial have come into proper directional position with the surrounding country, and any desired direction can be read off on the dial.

FIG. 21   *Swedish Orienteering Compass*

USING THE MAGNETIC COMPASS
WITHOUT DECLINATION

Emphasis has been placed in the foregoing on the importance of considering compass declination. While it would be folly under circumstances of major travel not to apply compass declination, I wish to point out that if travel is to be in a small, rather localized area, methods for using the compass without applying declination can be used. One can also set off the declination for the entire local area by drawing a com-

pass-north line on the map and then proceeding to
travel in the area as though the compass needle were
actually showing true north.

In setting off declination for the whole local area
in this fashion, first orient the map so that it corresponds directionally with the land area around you,
the top of the map then being true north. Next, lay
the compass on the map so that the dial (not the
needle) of the compass corresponds with the true
directions of the map—the N and S on the compass
dial lining up with the north and south directions on
the map. Now draw a line on the map that is parallel
to the compass needle as it comes to rest in your
area. Remove the compass and draw another line
across the map at right angles to the first line. From
now on instead of using the true north and south on
the map, just pretend that the two lines are north,
south, east, and west, and use your compass in conjunction with these lines as though the needle pointed
true north. With this method you will seem to be
traveling without regard to true north, but actually
you have considered declination, because you applied it when you drew the two lines.

If no map at all is being used and we keep travel
localized in a small wilderness area, the compass can
be used without regard for true north and without
declination providing we do not associate certain
geographical aspects or specific points of the area
with a true-north reference but use the compass-
north direction entirely. We get a clearer view of this
simplified method for local travel if theoretically we
erase all directions and calibrations on the compass
dial and simply travel according to how the needle
comes to rest directionally. We could—and still make

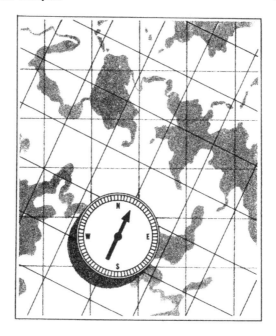

FIG. 22 *Setting Off Compass Declination with Simple Grid Lines*

sense—for example, mark the cardinal points on the dial: A, B, C, D, or 1, 2, 3, 4—even forward, back, right, and left, or any other arbitrary designation, disregarding standard directional terms in favor of these arbitrary markings. Then, if we gave directions to someone we could simply say, "travel in compass direction A one mile, then in compass direction B one mile, and so on, or direction 1, direction 2, and so forth.

It is readily seen how the use of the compass by

the novice where he knows nothing about declination has enabled him to travel in a small area and come out fairly well, providing he did not wander very far out of his local area.

The risk involved in using this system of not applying declination is that reference may at the time, or later, be made to some point on a true directional basis rather than to compass north, with consequent confusion. Also, we may travel out of the particular local area far enough to have a changed compass declination and thus create still further confusion.

I found the method of not using declination valuable only in a very localized area where I directed a number of inexperienced people on a wilderness search with maps and compasses to find a lost person. Not having time in the emergency to explain compass declination, I simply pointed to the two magnetic grid lines I had drawn and told them to use their compasses in such a manner that the compass needle would correspond with the grid lines and as though these grid lines were running true north, south, east, and west.

In the final analysis, I think it is preferable—unless we are just exploring the back forty—to acquire the habit of always setting off compass declination and using standard true directions, as competent wilderness men, surveyors, and explorers do, so that all points on a map in common with conventional terms make sense with everything, everybody, everywhere. It will be of interest to the reader that the U.S. Coast and Geodetic Survey publishes charts from which the declination can be estimated for any time or place in the United States.

Perhaps it should be mentioned that any compass

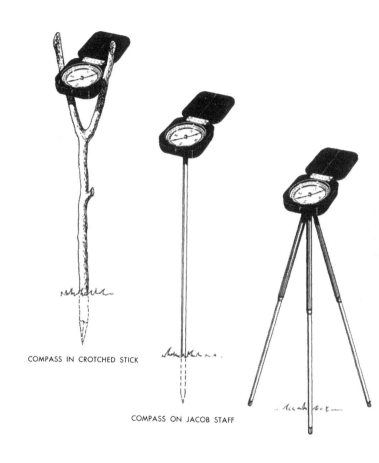

COMPASS IN CROTCHED STICK

COMPASS ON JACOB STAFF

COMPASS ON CAMERA TRIPOD

FIG. 23 *Compass Supports*

held in the hand and sighted for a bearing can, at best, give only a rough direction or bearing. A finely calibrated compass mounted on a camera tripod or a

Jacob staff (a stick with a tripod head) is necessary
for accurate bearings and triangulation work. For
want of either, use a stump, a crotched stick stuck
in the ground, or other available support. A fine,
well-calibrated compass is a valuable asset, and the
best type of magnetic compasses are relatively inexpensive.

SPECIAL NONMAGNETIC-TYPE COMPASSES

THE ASTROCOMPASS (SOLAR COMPASS)

There are places where a magnetic compass has a
minimal value, or none at all, such as the region in
the vicinity of the magnetic poles. We must then
resort to an astrocompass, where exact bearings are
taken from the sun or stars (see Appendix, page 200,
for its use). With the astrocompass we get true bearings, with no concern for declination.

THE GYROCOMPASS

The gyrocompass, requiring electric power, is too
cumbersome in weight and size for the wilderness
traveler except in flight or aboard heavier-type watercraft. The gyrocompass, though preset at the beginning of a voyage, is sometimes reset along the route
for directional correction by observations on heavenly bodies with an astrocompass.

THE POLARIZED SKY COMPASS

The polarized sky compass, sometimes called a
twilight compass, is an instrument that can be used

FIG. 24 *Astrocompass*

for directional reference during twilight and when the sun is near or even a few degrees below the horizon but obscured by clouds, provided that the overhead sky is clear. The greatest use of the polarized compass is in the polar regions, where the magnetic compass cannot be relied upon because of radical declinations or where it becomes useless, and when in winter the sun at its highest point hovers near or just below the horizon. Those who desire information on the polarized sky compass can find it treated at length in Hydrographic Office Publication 216, from the Superintendent of Documents, U.S. Government Printing Office, Washington, D.C. 20402. The instru-

FIG. 25 *Polarized Sky Compass*

ment is small enough to be portable for wilderness travel and should, of course, be considered by serious arctic expedition groups.

CHAPTER FIVE

Relating Our Route to Something Else

ANY CONSIDERATION of wilderness route finding must be reckoned on the basis of its relation to something else—a known reference factor that can be applied to our own approximate or unknown position. Strangely, this process of relating to something else—the most important element in route finding—is generally the most overlooked.

Our immediate position on the trail or route as it relates to a *line of position*—the "something-else" factor—is our first concern. This line of position can be one of various kinds of compass lines to be considered herein, or it can also, as we shall see in a later chapter, be determined by a simple sextant sight on the sun, a star, or other conveniently positioned body in the sky.

If you can imagine standing in the center of a compass, a line from you to every degree on the compass and on to a geographical point or the horizon could be a compass line of position. When you are sighting on a body somewhat low in the sky, for a simple direction only, a line from you through that body would be a line of position.

Also, a line of position could be a geographical

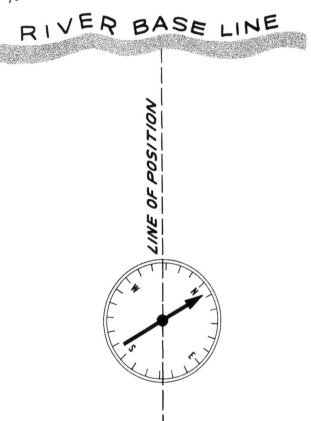

FIG. 26   *Compass Line of Position*

line of any kind, from a visible point of any kind to another point. Or, a line of position could be the many lines referred to herein as base lines, if such lines finally intersect other base lines.

A line of position, however it is determined, should in the truest sense of its own definition be regarded as just that: a *position line* on which you are located or traveling—not a fixed point of position. Basically, in all route-finding procedure, we assume to be traveling along a position line of some kind until we reach a predetermined base line, and then we travel along this base line until it brings us to a particular destination point.

We might even consider some lines of position and base lines, in so elementary a sense, as being analogous to traveling in a city along an avenue (a line of position), continuing until we reach a certain street intersection (a base line), when in turn we direct our travel to a particular point—a house or business address.

The only real distinction, then, to be made here between lines of position and base lines is that we move along compass or other lines of position toward known established intersecting base lines, such as rivers, railroads, lake shores, seacoasts, roads, and so forth. As in the chapter on maps and map reading, we might also compare position lines and base lines with surveyed township and range lines; or meridians and base lines; or even with so simple an analogy in map work as north-south, east-west lines, or as vertical and horizontal lines. The really important factor to remember is that in most instances we need to have our position lines and base lines intersect. Certain few exceptions, where these lines require no intersections, will be shown later.

But no matter what the nature of our travel, we are never wholly independent directionally. As indicated in Chapter 1, we can never be alien to our

surroundings or to an instrument of some kind if we
are to find our way without trial and error. As stated,
we have no innate sense of direction, and for this
reason in order to maintain a systematic orientation,
we must always relate ourselves to *something else*.
That something else can be anything apart from our
own being no matter what it is, just so long as it has
some directional or positional value for us. That
something else can be a compass line of position
along which we travel toward a base line. That something else can be an indefinite route of travel in an
unknown area toward a broad base line, such as a
road, railroad, mountain range, lake shore, river, and
so forth, along which, in turn, we can travel to a
particular destination point. But always and without
exception, we must relate ourselves to something
else. No matter how independent we profess to be
where orientation in wilderness travel is concerned, if
we are to move with any degree of sustained accuracy, we must, figuratively speaking, always be tied
to the apron strings of that something else.

Lines of position drawn on a map over land or
water are best made with the straight edge of a light
10- or 12-inch plastic protractor, after the compass
direction has been laid out on the protractor's radius.
The protractor thus becomes an important and valuable accessory to the map and compass in our route-
finding program. If map sections are cemented to
⅛-inch marine plywood, or to what is called hard-
board, and carried in a waterproof fabric envelope,
the protractor can conveniently be carried with the
maps. Use hard, sharp-pointed pencils for drawing
position lines. Thick lead pencil points make hazy
intersection points.

In addition to line of position, base line, and destination point, we have a fourth factor to consider: the *time/distance element.* For example, if we know our general rate of travel in a given compass direction, we can roughly designate our position from one point to another by checking the duration of travel. I say roughly because we are not likely to fix our exact position either on land or sea to any high degree of accuracy only by a time-and-direction method, because we cannot always sustain uniform travel over rough country or on a heavy sea. Nevertheless, a route-finding theory generally requires that we first roughly guess what our position is. As it were, "rough it in" by any means that we have at hand, theoretical or otherwise, no matter how general or vague the estimate of that rough position happens to be. In short, we must assume a general position in order eventually to calculate a particular position. (Even the highest form of celestial navigation at sea is calculated on a roughly assumed position, as a basis for determining an exact position.)

Where travel is on foot, we can roughly precheck our average rate of travel over known distances and kind of country with a pedometer, a watchlike instrument carried upright in a watch pocket or hooked onto the trouser belt. The pedometer mechanism operates on a rocker-arm-and-spring principle, the impact of every step causing the rocker-arm to descend and alternately spring back, moving a ratchet wheel which tallies the steps and totals the miles covered by the wearer. The length of step for each individual is easily preset on the pedometer by an adjustment assembly, somewhat in the same fashion as we might regulate the slow or fast escapement-control mechanism of a watch.

The pedometer designed for a man can also be

FIG. 27 *Pedometer*

adapted to a pack or saddle horse, sled dog, camel, or other animal, providing a test mile is made to learn what the pedometer will read over the mile for the particular animal. No matter what the reading shows for an animal in a test mile, that reading can be used as a multiplying factor for computing the entire distance traveled by the animal.

We can now consider line of position, base line, destination point, and the time/distance element as they apply to wilderness travel. Suppose, for example, that a small prospecting party has established a base camp by plane on the north shore of Great Bear Lake in the Yukon Territory of Canada or on the shore of some other large wilderness body of water. The party, we shall assume, intends to leave the shore base camp and travel on foot to a prospecting destination north of the lake. The route will be a north compass route drawn on the map to destination point, but the roughness of the terrain and the need to circumvent rather large natural barriers will not allow the party to travel a straight line. Rather, the route will have to be through an imaginary corridor, over a meandering trail that crosses and recrosses a compass line of position (see Fig. 28). The straight compass line of position itself is assumed to be somewhere roughly as close toward the center of the meandering trail and the corridor as possible. A constant check by the compass man at every important deviation to the right or left from the direct compass route will give a fair estimate of how far the party wavers in the detours from the main compass line of position, as the diagram will show. Each deviation from the main compass line of position will require

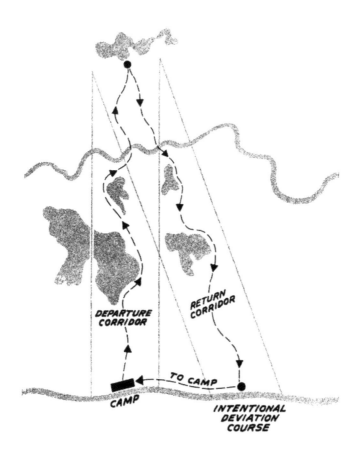

DEPARTURE CORRIDOR

RETURN CORRIDOR

TO CAMP

CAMP

INTENTIONAL DEVIATION COURSE

FIG. 28   *Departure-and-Return Corridor*

a particular compass bearing (direction). The distance from each deviation point will have to be estimated by duration of travel, or the distance ascertained by pedometer, or when possible designated by landmark. This is shown more particularly in Figure

FIG. 29   *Compass Bearings*

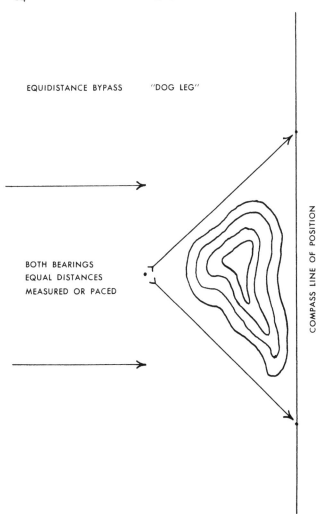

FIG. 30   *Equidistant Bypass (Dog-Leg) Angle*

29. The bypasses around geographical obstacles can be made as shown in Figure 28; or for greater accuracy, should be made as shown in Figure 30. When this is not feasible, the bypasses can be made as shown in Figure 29.

When the party has finished its work at the end of the operation and plans to return to the base on Great Bear Lake, it cannot, as shown in Figure 28, simply reverse the direction of its outgoing route and expect to return over the same general route to the base camp, unless of course the route happens to be well punctuated along the way with conspicuous landmarks, since the numerous compass bearings taken for the deviations along the route will likely be too general for such accuracy. Great Bear Lake being such a vast body of water (about 200 miles east to west), when the party reached its north-shore base line again, because of the likely side-drift error on the return trail, the party on arriving at some uncertain lakeshore point would have no idea which direction along the shore to travel to reach the base camp.

There are several methods the party can pursue on the return route. One method, as shown in Figure 28, is to return over a newly selected compass line of position that by an *intentional-deviation error* would be sure to strike the shore of the lake either to the east of the base camp or to the west of it, depending upon which side was selected for ease of travel as the best possible deviation-return route. The party thus having returned to the lake by a route of intentional error at a predetermined side of the base camp would then know which direction along the shore to travel in order to reach the base camp.

Another method for returning to the lake camp

from the inland prospecting mission is based on a
system of landmark safety brackets. After the party
is first deposited by plane on the shore of Great Bear
Lake and before the plane departs, the party uses the
plane to set up two or more shore landmarks—one
at each side of the base camp. These can be conspicuously blazed trees; bright, luminous cloth mark-
ers; rock mounds; or they can be natural landmarks,
if the landmarks can easily be seen and identified.
Such landmarks should be placed along the shore a
mile to the right and left of the camp. Another set
of landmarks should be placed on each side at 5
miles. If the prospecting area to be worked north of
the camp is extremely broad, say several hundred
miles, then bracket landmarks should be as far as 10
miles, or even more, along the shore on each side
of the base camp.

The purpose of this bracketing-in system will be
obvious. When the prospecting party takes its bearing before returning to the lake, it can disregard the
deviation route back previously described and travel
over the most conveniently direct compass line of
position to the lake, moving off this position line
only as the rough contour requires. When the party
reaches the lake, it will be safely bracketed in by the
shore landmarks. Landmarks or camp may not be
seen on arriving at the lake, but no matter which
direction along the shore the compass man travels to
determine the party's position, he will come upon one
of the bracket landmarks. Information, of course,
will have been placed in or on the landmarks to
designate the direction of the camp, or descriptive
identifying notes of the landmarks will have been
made beforehand to give this information.

It will become apparent that on leaving any base line in areas of forest, tundra, prairie, or desert, the system of bracketing-in the base line to which one returns allows free movement over a rather general area.

If we apply the bracketing principle to other areas, say on an east-west auto road, dirt road, logging road, railroad, etc., where the party plans to investigate a wild area north of the road, bracket landmarks could be established on the road both to the right and to the left of the point of departure from the road. If, for example, the party had arrived at the point of departure by car, jeep, or other vehicle, it is important to drive up and down the road a short distance until some kind of bracket landmarks can be sighted and established visually or manually. In the case mentioned earlier, the hunter who failed to find his car on a tote road, needed to widely bracket-in the position of his car on the road with landmarks before he left it to travel north from the tote road. He would then have been what we might term "safety-curbed" on his return between the bracketed landmarks.

Thus, we can see that no matter where we travel, whether it be in a semiwild area of auto roads, tote roads, and railroads or a primitive wilderness, when we leave a base line, the base line should be bracketed. Such bracketing can be applied visually or manually to any base line, road, railroad, lake shore, seacoast, mountain range, river, canyon, arroyo— even, as we shall see later, a compass line of position established by sighting a distant point such as a mountain peak or a line of position sighted with a sextant on the sun or a star (see Fig. 31).

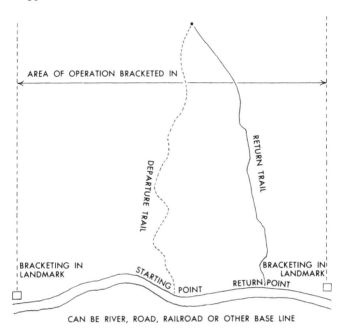

AREA OF OPERATION BRACKETED IN

RETURN TRAIL

DEPARTURE TRAIL

BRACKETING IN
LANDMARK

STARTING POINT

BRACKETING IN
LANDMARK

RETURN POINT

CAN BE RIVER, ROAD, RAILROAD OR OTHER BASE LINE

FIG. 31   *Establishing Landmark Safety Brackets*

Getting back to our Great Bear Lake examples, if there should be prominent landmarks visible on the original outgoing course away from the lake, certain to be visible on the return route of travel, there would, of course, be no problem in returning along the outgoing route. It is not always possible to travel from landmark to landmark unless they are prominent and frequent—a general compass line of position most often being required. But whenever it is possible to identify a few such landmarks, naturally they form valuable aids for redirecting and consequently shortening the return compass course, because the amount of intentional-deviation error heretofore described could then be reduced. Or, the described system of bracket landmarks along the shore base line could be greatly narrowed. On extensive travel, only large and conspicuous landmarks which are visible on both the going and the coming routes should be considered. Small, inconspicuous landmarks difficult to identify from another angle or which become obscured from vision on our return tend only to confuse. (Most of us have heard the anecdote about the man who blazed his outgoing trail through a forest on the near side of trees, and on his return became lost because he could not see his concealed blaze marks from the opposite direction.)

Using landmarks for travel might suggest that we go from landmark to landmark. This is sometimes true, but we must also consider that convenient landmarks for travel can be long distances away and still be visible. They may be off to one side. They can, nevertheless, be just as valuable as those on our trail, because we use them not for immediate landmarks but for compass lines of position. (See Chapter 7, Lines of Position, for a comprehensive coverage of this subject.)

Now let us consider a third method which may be used in traveling from Great Bear Lake to the north and return. It is the triangulation method used by a forester in locating a fire, a principle warranting general description because it has a broad application for us.

In the fire observation tower high above the forest,

the forest ranger spots a column of smoke in the distance. Before him in the tower is a large, fixed, calibrated, compass dial, properly oriented in a directional position so that it does not need a magnetic needle. Instead of the compass needle, there is an arrow which can be rotated by hand and pointed at the distant fire. On the arrow are mounted sights or a magnifying scope with sighting cross hairs. This dial and arrow assembly is called a pelorus. (The forester could, of course, use an ordinary compass— the basic principle being the same.)

As the arrow is pointed at the fire, it will come to rest over one of the compass-dial degrees—any single calibration from 0 to 360. The forester in the tower reads off the tower-to-fire line of position and phones or radios it to headquarters. At headquarters there is a large wall map of the area, with strings that can be stretched as lines of position, fixed with thumbtacks from tower positions along the reported directional pelorus line of position to the fire. Or, the lines of position can also be drawn on a smaller map, using a protractor, a method now more commonly practiced.

So far, all that headquarters knows about the location of the fire is that it is somewhere on this line of position emanating from the observation tower. A fire-fighting plane could, of course, be flown close enough to the tower to sight the fire. But this indirect route to the fire would only waste valuable fire-fighting time. It is not necessary because the fire will be sighted from still another tower and from a different angle. This different line of position, too, is radioed to headquarters. The headquarters stretches another string on the map from the location of this second tower along the different, reported, pelorus line of position to the fire. Wherever these strings intersect (cross) on the map is the fixed position of the fire. It is now a simple matter for headquarters to create a third compass line of position with a string on the map stretched from headquarters to the exact fire location, and it will be along this third compass line of position from headquarters to the scene of the fire that the fire-fighting plane or overland crew will set its course to reach the fire (Fig. 32).

Thus, intersecting lines of position make what is termed a fix (a fixed position). Such adaptations of position lines determined by compass directions, as described, are called triangulation, and they provide a valuable basic principle in the general route-finding program—one, as I have indicated, deserving special consideration and emphasis here. (Also, see triangulation by using the null point of the common portable radio given later in this chapter.)

The prospecting party on Great Bear Lake could then, for this third example, employ a triangulation method in finding the base camp on the shore, providing there were distant islands or prominent points out in the lake or even distant mountain peaks or other land points on which to sight such position lines with a compass or transit from the camp or along the trail.

But before the prospecting party had originally departed from the lake base camp for the northern prospecting mission, they would have had to fix the relative position of the camp on the lake shore by sighting from the camp with a compass or transit on

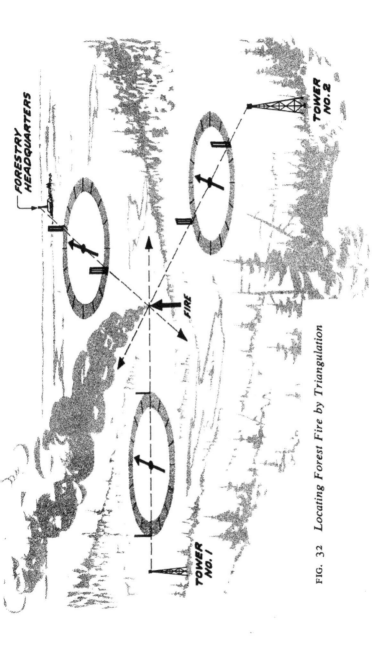

FIG. 32 Locating Forest Fire by Triangulation

FIG. 33A   *Compass Lines to Mountain Peak and Island*

one or more of the geographical features as reference points. These islands, land points, or mountain peaks would, of course, have to be visible for sighting a line of position anywhere along a rather extensive, general segment of the base-camp shoreline, wherever the party happened to arrive, to be of practical value.

A lake can have a number of fairly similar islands and points of land that might create confusion if seen from a strange segment of shore east or west of the camp. This problem can be resolved by taking a number of compass readings from the base camp to various islands and points. A combination of sighted compass directions, or bearings, as they are called, from the base camp to these islands or points of land will form an identifiable, triangulation *pattern* of position lines that by the law of probability is not likely to reoccur directionally anywhere along the entire shoreline. If another pattern of triangulation lines is sighted at the return point on the lake, east or west of the camp, a comparison of the two patterns and a bit of common-sense deduction will generally designate the camp's position relative to the arrival point on the lake from the north.

Most islands and points of land, however, have special features that tend to distinguish and thus identify them, although such distinguishing features sometimes change in appearance, as previously suggested, when seen from various angles. A pocket notebook and pencil are essential for tabulating the various compass directions from the camp to the islands, and it is also a good policy to describe with brief, identifying notes for later reference various features of the islands and points when they are being initially sighted with the compass. Such factors should never be left to memory.

While triangulation requires two or more compass sights to fix a position, if we examine the lake-shore illustration, we will see that the location of the camp on the shore could also be determined by a single compass line of position from the camp to an identifiable, distant point. In other words, there is no other place along the north shore that the camp could possibly be located except on one single, specific compass line of position from the camp to the identified distant island, mountain peak, or a particularly prominent tree on a distant hill, or any other point.

The return route to Great Bear Lake from the inland prospecting area, used in our example, would not, if we were able to use the triangulation method or the single compass sight just described, have to be the intentional-deviation error east or west from the north-south compass line of departure as suggested in our first example. Rather, in the triangulation method, as in the bracketing plan, a return route as close as possible along the departure north-and-south compass line could be followed, because on returning to the lake-shore base line, no confusion should arise as to which direction along the shore the camp was situated. The triangulation method, or a simple compass reading to the distant identified island, point, or mountain peak, when the prospectors reached any part of the lake shore would give the arrival position on the lake shore relative to the base camp.

Obviously, this use of triangulation will also apply

to positions other than waterfronts. On the desert, prairie, tundra, or out on large open water, for example, two or more available compass sights to known, visible, elevated objectives, such as distant mesas, rims, mountain peaks, lake points, or islands, identified on the map, will serve to fix a position. Where a single compass sight happens to intersect a river, lake shore, or any other known available line, this sight alone will also fix a position.

If mountain peaks visible in the distance cannot be identified on the map but can be distinguished enough from others for our own designation, they can, by the triangulation method, serve to fix a position point to which we can return.

Even a single, distant, known, visible peak or other prominence will provide a compass line of position that can be followed to a return point, just so long as we know which direction along the compass line to travel. A compass line to a distant peak or other visible point can also have the described bracket landmarks aplied to it as a base line to which we can return.

Where the terrain is such that no distant, conspicuous mountain peak or other elevated reference landmark can be seen for triangulation purposes or for a single line of position over which to travel, our course would, as described earlier, be by a compass line of position to a known or established base line. In short, it is essential to travel along a compass line of position to a base line rather than to depend on traveling along a compass line of position to a fixed point. There is always a grave risk when the compass line of position is not determined by a distant, con-

FIG. 33B   *Two Compass Sights to Known Mountain Peaks Fix a Position by Triangulation*

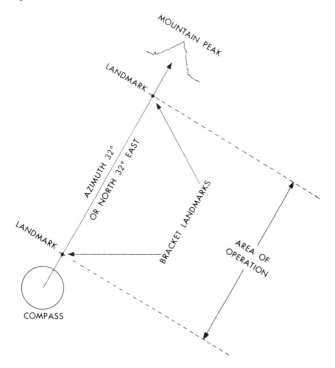

FIG. 34   *Bracket on Compass Line*

tinually visible point, such as a mountain peak or
other prominence, that our destination along a compass line of position might be bypassed. For this
reason under such circumstances we should for
safety's sake return from a wild area to the broad
expanse of any available base line, preferably to a
bracketed base line.

On desert, prairie, tundra, and sea ice, small monuments or mounds on the highest available elevations

should be erected with rocks, dirt, or ice as focal points from which compass lines of position or base lines can emanate. Sometimes these monuments are topped with bright strips of cloth easily seen from considerable distances especially if cloth with luminous dye is used. Binoculars of the small pocket size in 7- or 8-power should be part of the equipment when these flagged monuments are used, in order that the monuments may be seen at sufficient distances to minimize their number. A variety of colors in luminous cloth strips, each color having a particular meaning, can be used for identification, the colors indicating relative distances, direction, and so on.

This kind of route marking, using snow monuments, has been found valuable by various exploration parties and the military on the Greenland Ice Cap. On the tundra, desert, and prairie, use rocks or dirt, if natural prominences are not available.

We cannot stress too much the importance of identifying each individual monument in a notebook, giving the compass bearing to a point on the back trail, the compass bearing to a point on the trail ahead, the date and the time of day it was last visited. Also, it is important to describe in detail any geographical formations in the immediate vicinity that can be used as relative factors in identifying the position of the monument.

Waterproof, waxed crayon, or timber cruiser's graphite crayon can be used for position marking on the rocks of monuments if the monuments are not to be used over too long a time, since weather might eventually obliterate the markings. Where monuments need long-duration marking, the data should be written on paper and folded in foil, then buried in

FIG. 35 *Compass Lines of Position to and from a Monument*

dirt or properly weighted down against heavy winds.

The marking of monuments can be reduced to a minimum if the monuments are numbered or lettered for identification and the data tabulated in a pocket notebook. But such code systems of identification do not help strange travelers or give knowledge to subsequent expeditions coming upon your monuments. Due also to the possible loss of notebooks in arduous travel, the data is best placed both on the monument and in a notebook. Careful work of this kind makes for competence in exploration travel and contributes to a fine historical tradition. Where notes are buried in foil, a corner of the foil should appear above the ground if information is to be imparted to those who come afterward.

The reader will see the uncertainty and risk involved in traveling from point to point—that is, monument to monument—as compared with travel from a monument over a compass line of position to a base line. In short, we should take advantage of every natural position line or base line in the region, even if it necessitates a little additional travel—sometimes even an appreciable amount. Travel from a monument over a compass line of position to a river base line, for instance, then along the river to another monument or landmark can be a more certain combination than travel from monument to monument, unless, as I have indicated, monuments or other landmark points can be seen from considerable distances. The bypass danger is always imminent. Even when a monument is established on a compass line of position, say to a mountain peak, the weather could be such that poor visibility might hide the monument and thus impair the position line.

It must also be remembered that the risk of missing an objective point such as a monument or other single, isolated point rather than a base line increases in direct ratio to the distance traveled.

As we shall see in Chapter 8, we can establish east-west lines of position with rather simple sextant sights on the sun or the Pole Star. By using such east-west lines as lines of position sighted with a sextant, in conjunction with intersecting base lines that have been established with monuments, we can make travel on the tundra, prairie, and desert a rather positive process.

In rough country it may be necessary to set up a series of monuments to establish a long enough line of position or base line. At least enough monuments should be established to prevent any possible bypass on the return route. Monuments must also be situated close enough together and at such strategic points in forming a position line or base line that they can be seen from each successive monument or from any low point between them. When one approaches a base line, a monument should be visible off in the distance to the right or to the left to avoid a bypass. The monument should be visible at least with field glasses, but preferably with the naked eye.

It will become obvious to the reader that various natural features can also be used in place of monuments or in addition to them, such as a salient cliff, mesa, hill, high rock—any prominence that can be easily and *positively identified and distinguished from others* or accessibly marked with luminous cloth strips and conspicuously seen.

Travel along or in the region of a river often simplifies the route-finding problem if the river can be set up in the plan of travel either as a line of position or as a base line; but not all rivers, we must remember, are linear, channeled currents flowing between embankments. Many rivers, as on the Pre-Cambrian Shield in Canada, for example, are a series of lakes or other expansions, ranging from ponds to vast marshes, or even freshwater seas of a hundred miles or more, connected by short or long stretches of channeled rivers. Also, one lake might drop to another water level by an abrupt waterfall or cataract without a segment of channeled river between them. Canoe routes through waters with such irregular shores and deep bays can become involved. The delta of the Mackenzie River is an example of a complex, ramified water area, especially at certain times of the year when the seasonal water level could change markedly during the going-and-coming period of travel.

In relating our route to that something else, perhaps one of the most unusual factors in modern-day route finding is the inherent directional and position-fixing principle of radio. Travel by radio beacon is well known at sea and in the air, using heavy equipment, but we should not overlook the fact that this principle can also be applied to wilderness route finding by tuning the extremely portable, common transistor radio to any conventional broadcast station.

The fortunate route-finding principle of the common radio is that, with its built-in loop antenna, reception becomes directional—though in a rather strange way. We get no directional value, for instance, from the broadcast sound itself; but as we slowly rotate the radio away from its loudest receiving position, we reach a null point at each end of

the radio. These are dead spots where a minimum or
no reception comes through. One end, or the other,
of the radio (not the tuning face or the back) will
then be directed toward the broadcast station. Where
we do not know our own position, we cannot at first
determine from these reciprocal null points alone,
which null point end of the radio points to the station. This can, however, be ascertained by later
procedure.

What we do have, for a start, is a line of position
on which an unknown broadcast station and the
observer with his portable radio are situated. With a
compass, map, and lead pencil, this position line
can be set down on the map, as the procedure will
presently show.

Before this position line is drawn, reception needs
to be brought in for identification (not direction) of
the radio broadcast station, unless the identity of the
station is already known. While a method for learning the direction of the station will be given in the
following procedure, we are not usually so completely disoriented in our presumed position area
that we fail to know our general position relative to
a distant station.

Procedure:

After the station has been identified from its own
broadcast, use a compass to place the map in its true
north-south position, using the side edges of the map
for reference. Chapter 4, The Compass, will provide
information on true, rather than magnetic, "north."
Maps showing the fixed points of broadcast stations

can be had from The Department of Aeronautics for the region of travel, or general maps can be used to mark in the position of needed stations.

Thus, with the map directionally in position, set either the front or back, bottom edge of the radio on the indicated position of the broadcast station; hold it on the station, and slowly rotate the radio until it aligns with the null point. A sharp lead pencil line drawn through the indicated point of the broadcast station and along the already directionally positioned straight edge of the radio establishes your line of position. You are somewhere on this line. If the position line, because of a distant station, needs to be extended over a large map area, this can easily be done by stretching a black thread parallel with the drawn position line.

Now, if another broadcast station off toward right angles to the first radio position line is selected, and the same step-by-step procedure is followed for another line of position, where these lines cross, your fixed position will be there. Here again we have a basic triangulation principle.

A strip of one-eighth inch marine plywood placed under the map gives a smooth and flat surface in the wilderness for drawing and extending the pencil lines of position.

If you do not know which end of the radio is pointing toward the broadcast station, you can determine this by another radio observation on one or both of the same two broadcast stations farther along your route of travel. If the angle between your direction of travel and a radio line of position increases, the broadcast station is fore. If the angle decreases, it is aft. Such common sense deductions will tell whether the stations are, broadly speaking, ahead, behind, to the right, or left.

Travel by plane, watercraft, snowmobile, saddle horse, jeep, or on foot is often toward or away from towns having radio broadcast stations, or from one station across a wilderness area to another station. While positions can, of course, be fixed from time to time in the intervening wilderness area with radio observations as described, movement toward and away from towns having radio stations can usually be made merely by keeping the null point fixed on the station, no matter how zigzag the course. Because of a null point at each end of the radio, the observer needs to know roughly his general direction from the station, and should accompany his radio with a compass for determining this presumed position. To be sure that the radio is continuously giving off a null point, it is necessary only to turn the radio off course momentarily for the broadcast sound to come in and resume course again by picking up the null point.

Even though radio reception is better at night, it gives rough null points from about a half hour before sunset to a half hour after sunrise. Where travel by water has to be extended into the night, it would be well to fix one's position beforehand with the more accurate daytime null points, and continue travel by compass course, or use other position finding methods at night. (See sextant sights on stars in Chapter 8.) Most wilderness land and water travel being in daylight, the night null-point problem can be considered negligible.

Metal on powered watercraft can cause deviation

of null points. Therefore, the radio should be moved about in the craft by trial and error until the best null points are obtained, the null points then tested on a directionally known broadcast station before travel proceeds.

High intervening land masses can cause deviation of null points. On land, therefore, observations should be made from the highest accessible elevation. On water, they should be made well away from shore.

Radio stations nearest the observer give the least errors; that is, more accurate null points than very distant stations. Nearer stations also allow cutting down the size of the map, thus reducing the length of position lines. While vest-pocket-size radios can be used in wild areas proximal to a broadcast station, travel in remote wilderness regions calls for a portable radio of greater range and selectivity. The latter can be had in prices ranging from $50 to $200, with no certainty that the costliest or those with the greatest number of transistors will be best. All radios should be tested for satisfactory null points and range before purchase. Degree of care in focusing null points determines accuracy of position.

Because the use of radio lines of position can be regarded as a wholly independent route-finding method, complemented, of course, by the incidentals of map, compass, protractor, and pencil, the radio procedure here has been considered separately from the various other component line-of-position methods given in this book. Nevertheless, the astute reader will at once see the importance of using individual radio lines of position in conjunction with all other lines of position obtained by different methods, treated in this and other chapters. Combining them not only increases the value of radio position lines themselves, but also broadens the entire scope of route-finding procedure.

A radio line of position, for example, can fix an actual position in the wilderness, as basically described for other methods, where the radio line crosses such position lines as a lake shore, river, tote road, railroad, highway, seacoast, canyon, arroyo, etc. The radio line of position can fix a position where it is used to intersect a compass line of position sighted to a mountain peak, island, point of a headland, or other object that will serve as a visible compass bearing. A radio line of position can even be used to intersect a latitude line of position, the latter easily obtained by the layman with a simple sextant sight on a star or the sun—extending to him a combination form of radio and celestial navigation greatly simplified over the longer conventional methods of complex navigation. (For simple sextant sights on the sun and stars, see Chapters 7, 8, and Appendix, pages 174-181.)

Relating our route to something else obviously, then, includes a rather large category of tangible clues, some natural or instrumental; others, in a sense, hypothetical. The secret of successful route finding lies in acknowledging this interdependence on clues and the ability to complement our senses with every available orientation factor we can apply to the wilderness environment.

CHAPTER SIX

Natural Route Finders

WHILE THERE has been a tendency down through travel history to exaggerate the value of natural route-finding clues, we need to consider the advantages of practical ones: those which prove to be positive directional factors in an emergency and those used in conjuction with instruments.

First in order of importance, of course, are the "guideposts in the sky"—the sun and stars. On board ship a noon sextant observation of the sun for latitude has become traditional.

We are apt to be rather dogmatic about the more common directional use of the sun—the average individual considers loosely that it rises in the east and sets in the west. About March 21 (the vernal equinox) and about September 23 (the autumnal equinox), it definitely does rise in the east and set in the west, as is clear to the observer who views the rising and setting phenomena over water or a comparable land horizon. Over rough terrain the sun will not always appear to the observer as true east and west in its rising and setting, but for most travel the error will not be significant. Of course, during these equinoctial periods, the sun cannot be seen in the polar regions.

On the sun's annual journey north of the equator, it reaches a point over the earth's surface about June 22 (the summer solstice) at approximately 23.4 degrees north latitude. Then it moves southward until it reaches a point over the earth's surface about December 22 (the winter solstice) at approximately 23.4 degrees south latitude. Depending upon where we are situated at this time of year, we will find the sun's directional position in relation to our own varying considerably away from an east rising and west setting—and also, of course, varying directionally throughout the day as it arcs over the sky.

We can obtain from the Government Printing Offices a set of so-called azimuth (direction) tables that will show the exact direction of the sun within one-tenth of a degree from any position we assume on the earth for every moment of each day in the year. But such tables must be computed by the altitude of a heavenly body at a particular time. And such computations are not likely to be at hand in some unforeseen circumstance when we are compelled to use only the sun without instruments as an emergency directional guide. We should, therefore, commit to memory the sun's approximate directional position throughout the year.

These rough approximations are not difficult when we observe that in June the sun rises and sets far to the north of east and west, and in December far to the south of east and west. If, then, in June and December we observe the sun's direction with a compass or note the north-and-south variations away from true east risings and west settings at the region of intended travel, no difficulty should

be experienced in making a rough memory estimate
of approximately where the sun will rise and set
during the intermediate months. We know that the
sun rises and sets due east and west about March 21
and September 23. We also know that it requires 3
months to change its setting position from *true* east
and west to its most extreme point north of east and
west, and 3 months to change from its extreme setting point south of *true* east and west. Somewhere in
between these two extremes, our estimate will determine at other times of the year approximately where
from our own position, the sun will rise and set.

The sun light-spot and sun shadow-tip methods of
determining the sun's position, illustrated for years
in various children's camp manuals, make excellent
novelty exercises for children and, for that matter,
adults. But these methods have relatively little value
in a serious route-finding program except as emergency survival measures and should be learned only
for this contingency. Most of these methods are
based on creating light spots or stick shadow tips on
the rough ground, then waiting for hours while the
sun changes its position, so that later light spots or
shadow tips can complement the first ones to establish a direction.

The light-spot theory has been graphically illustrated if we have ever been in a shed where a knot
has fallen out of a wallboard, allowing the sun to
throw a light spot on the floor. Roughly speaking,
about March 21 and September 23 the light spot
will describe a straight east-west line across the floor.
Toward June 22 and December 22 the light spot will
describe a concave or convex arc. Of course, the

same principle will apply with a stick set in the
ground, a needle or straw mounted on a block of
wood, or any other device used to throw a shadow.
All are essentially rough procedures.

In actual practice, such processes are time con-
suming and of minimal value to the outdoorsman,
but the following methods are given in case of
emergency:

Insert a sheet of birch bark or other flat material
into a split stick and make a small hole, about ¼
inch or larger in diameter, just above the split stick.
Push the stick into the ground or prop it up with
stones so that the flat side of the bark sheet faces
the sun and creates a shadow area to throw a light
spot on level ground. Some time before noon measure the distance from the sun light spot to the base

FIG. 36 *Stake—Sun Shadow for Direction*

of the supporting stick. This A.M. measurement can be made with another stick. When the sun has made some progress over the sky after noon, make repeated measurements from the sun light spot to the base of the supporting stick until the P.M. sun light-spot measurement to the stick base is the same as the A.M. sun light-spot measurement to the stick base. Draw a line between these two marks on the ground. It will roughly be east-west.

It will be obvious to the reader that this same principle will apply to various shadow-tip methods shown in young people's publications.

Another method is to place a straight stick or pencil in the ground, slanting it toward the sun so that it will not cast a shadow. Then wait for a time until it does cast a short shadow. The length of this shadow will roughly be east-west. The method has some advantage as a time-saver over the longer dragged-out shadow-stick methods of limited value.

These sun light-spot and shadow-tip novelties can possibly be useful in survival emergencies but should be minimized in any serious route-finding program. If the reader is interested in expanding the use of the sun for taking accurate bearings, he should learn the simple elements of using the astrocompass (solar compass), as referred to in Chapter 4 and in the Appendix, page 200, or investigate the solar attachment adapted to the light explorer's transit. The astrocompass sold in government surplus can be had at about one-tenth its original cost and will provide a great deal more practical and precise material of solar interest than can be had by rough shadow experiments with sticks in the ground.

An ordinary wristwatch or pocketwatch can be

used to give a rough north-south direction, but such
methods as are contained in some camp manuals of
pointing the hour hand at the sun and finding north
halfway between the hour hand and 12, should not be
taken too literally. Extreme errors, especially as one
approaches the equator, make the method a very in-
accurate one. Errors are reduced somewhat if the
watch, instead of being held level, is inclined so that
it lies horizontally tangent to the earth's curvature
at the equator. In northern latitudes the face is held
upward; in southern latitudes it is held downward
and must be viewed from below, the watch being
held overhead. If the watch is used before 6 A.M. or

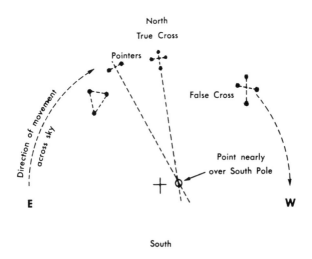

FIG. 37   *Southern Cross and Adjacent Stars Designating South-Polar Position*

after 6 P.M., the larger angle between the hour hand and 12—not the smaller angle—should be used.

The Pole Star, as we have indicated in Chapter 4, is a convenient directional point in the Northern Hemisphere. The disadvantage is that while night travel on water is possible, night travel on land over rough terrain for safety reasons is generally limited. The Pole Star can, at most, be only about 1 degree off from true north (see Polar Distance, pages 175-176 in Appendix). As explained in Chapter 4, the best time for determining true north is when the star Alkaid is at a specific position either above or below the Pole Star. The two stars on the outer part of the Dipper's cup point to the Pole Star, offering ready identification. There are, however, many such pointer combinations of stars available for identifying the North Star. Examination of any star chart will show them. The great Northern Cross (Cygnus) is one of these.

DIRECTION FROM STARS IN SOUTHERN HEMISPHERE

Unfortunately, there is no South Pole Star. The south-polar point is situated in a somewhat blank area of sky often referred to as the Coal Sack. We must, therefore, use constellations of stars in the proximity of the South Pole as pointers only, to find the true position of the South Pole.

The Southern Cross serves as our most important guide in designating this south-polar position. The Southern Cross consists of four stars, and we must be careful not to confuse it with a secondary or false

Southern Cross having five stars (see any star chart).

The rather bright stars that form the longest axis of the true Southern Cross point toward the south-polar position. To the east of the Southern Cross are two additional pointing stars that prove helpful in designating the polar position. The accompanying sketch will best show how the two intersecting lines (drawn with the eye or with a pencil on the star chart) from these two combinations of stars designate the south-polar point at their intersection, which proves the simple rule that two intersecting lines, by triangulation, fix an exact point; in this instance, the south-polar point.

The star Mintaka (Orionis Delta) has importance in the Southern Hemisphere for direction finding because it lies almost on the equator. Over water it can be seen to rise close to due east and set close to due west from any point on the earth except the polar regions, where it cannot be seen at all. At right angles to Mintaka when it rises or sets over water will be an approximate north-south directional line. Actually, it is about one-third of a degree off the equator and, therefore, off a true east-west rising and setting; but only a precision observation with a transit would make this distinction. Mintaka is one of the stars on the Belt of Orion and can be identified as being that one of the three farthest from Sirius, the Dog Star. (For further information on Mintaka, see the Appendix, pages 177-180.)

When using a particular compass direction for travel over rough terrain, it is difficult to keep our eyes on the compass for constant bearings. Small lapel or wrist compasses with short, highly responsive needles and compasses with needles dampened in a stabilizing fluid can readily be checked for rough readings with only momentary pauses on the trail. These lapel or wrist compasses can thus be a valuable complement to the more precise and sensitive cruiser's compass.

Chances are, however, that once we have established an approximate compass route, we are more inclined to rely on the sun or, in overcast, open areas, perhaps to some degree on a steady wind, rather than continual compass observation for holding roughly to a general direction. Where greater accuracy over a route is needed, periodically and when possible we will be sighting with a compass to specific, distant, visible points and methodically picking up successive alignment points from each sighted objective.

Where we use the wind in part for holding a rough compass course, it is well to check the wind direction with a compass from time to time throughout the day, since a sudden and deceptive shift in wind direction is possible.

On tundra and sea ice in winter we can use the wind for holding a direction; or, better, we can take advantage of the systematic drift patterns of snow— multiple ridges, called sastrugi. These snow patterns are generally parallel with a wind that has been blowing for some time. The formation of sastrugi is a valuable directional clue. However, it is wise before taking off on a journey to observe and check with a compass the established directional formations of these patterns.

Winds generally are prevailing in the Arctic certain times of the year and lay down sastrugi patterns that are not difficult to use as rough directional guides. But carelessness in not observing the possible variations from occasional general wind shift and change in new locations over extended travel can be misleading.

Drift patterns of desert sand can also be used to advantage in maintaining a course, but here too we should not be dogmatic about the constancy of formations. We can well afford to spend a little time in observing with a compass, watch, or the sun the directional effects of the wind on the sand in the area of travel. When we set off on a journey, we should not place too much reliance on some of the general information passed off as foolproof concepts about sand or sastrugi formations; whenever possible, the time to study directional clues of any kind is before we need them.

Perhaps the greatest value of sastrugi, wind, and sand drift as directional factors comes during storms, because the use of a compass is greatly impaired when limited visibility does not allow the taking of distant bearing points. The direction of sastrugi underfoot, seen every moment when heads are bowed low to avoid the wind's blast or flying snow, is an invaluable directional aid. Proper goggles, of course, greatly facilitate matters—green glass in goggles being best for prolonged use.

Where prevailing winds blow over open water, the directional wash of waves against the hull of a craft, if it is well away from land, is a rough directional guide. Near land, however, such wash can be deceptive. The single factor of constant wave direction alone has made it possible for small craft to travel through the day quite far from coasts or over rather large areas of inland water with no other directional assistance than waves breaking against a particular part of the hull and an occasional compass check for possible change of wind direction.

Over water, triangulation can have a big advantage whenever there is good visibility. While curvature of the earth obscures a view of average-height shores a relatively short distance out to sea, very often there are high land promontories, identifiable on a map, which remain visible quite far offshore. A single, familiar prominence of this kind, sighted with a compass, can place the craft on a line of position that tells the operator a great deal about his general location. If he can see two such familiar land prominences a considerable distance apart (at approximately 90°), he can, by two compass sights, fix his position exactly, using the triangulation method.

The time/distance element can also be an important factor in the use of natural route finders. Small-craft operators traveling by wave direction in a prevailing wind can know their positions fairly well over a large wilderness water if only a direction and a time record is kept on the outward course of travel. A previous knowledge of one's craft and its speed against or with the varying degrees of wind velocity and direction will, of course, be necessary in order to compute the mileage factor advantageously.

The wind most often dies down with the setting sun. In travel over broad areas of wilderness water by canoe, I have waited for the calm of the night, setting out when the wind of the day had died and holding the canoe to a course by luminous compass or the stars and a time factor, thus scheduling arrival on a far shore at a portage trail well before sunrise —before the morning wind could again spring up to rile the water.

When we use the sun for maintaining a general compass course, we unconsciously manage in time to allow for its hourly directional change across the sky. If not, just an occasional compass or watch check on our direction for the sun's position is usually all that is required. When walking with the sun more or less at our back, our body shadow projected before us makes a more convenient guide than when walking toward the sun. Never stare directly into the sun.

As we continue our travel and reach geographically known points or such points as can be identified from a map, it is possible at times to recheck and correct the various assumed positions (also called dead-reckoning positions), revising them to exact positions. Any distinctive breaks in an otherwise uniform region (such as elevations, marsh, bog, and muskeg areas, kinds of forests and their boundaries, mesas, mountain peaks, arroyos, or waterfalls), so charted on a map, are often important identifying factors in fixing exact positions from time to time along the route of travel.

The identifying factors do not necessarily have to be exactly on the route of travel. They can be points far from the trail. For example, a distant mountain peak, say, 20 miles away and off to one side, that can be identified on the map, will have a compass bearing that intersects the line of travel. If the directional line of travel is indicated by a compass bearing on some other point ahead, the intersection of these lines will fix an exact position.

There can come a time when each of us who travels extensively in wilderness areas is *really* lost—when no manner of position lines, base lines, or other directional factors can be identified or used in getting us back, say, to a base camp. If we are lost in such a major fashion that we have missed our established known base line, our plan may have to be that of disregarding the hope of immediately finding the locally used base line and seeking a more distant one. In other words, we shall have to rely on such very general base lines as a distant coast, railroad, transcontinental road, or whatever remote base line we can finally reach by extended travel that will reroute us to a temporary relief center. The closest distant base line, regardless of direction, will probably have to be chosen, because once we reach rapid, common-carrier transportation, a roundabout trip to our base by air or other rapid transit is not of serious consequence.

Being seriously lost does not often happen; but a not uncommon situation of being temporarily lost, or, as we say in polite wilderness parlance, "temporarily dislocated," is leaving a base camp and somehow completely missing the location of the camp on our return effort. It may be that we have bypassed the camp or, by the complexity of our wanderings in the miscalculated pursuit of some routine objective, we cannot now determine even in the remotest manner from observing our surroundings or the compass in which direction our base camp lies.

If we have a compass available, the sun is shining,

or there is a prevailing wind to guide us, we can walk a systematic pattern that will eventually bring the camp into view. The pattern to walk is a series of squares. In other words, we walk in a particular direction for a given length of time or a certain number of paces; then we turn at a right angle and walk the same time or number of paces continuing the right angle turns until we complete a square, carefully examining the region within and adjacent to the square for sight of the camp. Needless to say, these four sides of the square should be completed with as much accuracy and calm as possible, for life itself could under some circumstances depend on it. If the camp does not come into view, a larger and still larger square will have to be walked until the camp eventually does come into the pattern, for it must inevitably do so under this plan. Each succeeding square should not visually be so far removed from the previous one as to endanger bypassing the camp.

Better than a series of squares is the pattern shown in Figure 38. This can, however, become a bit confusing in times of stress unless you keep your wits about you. In this pattern a certain number of paces are walked, a right angle turn made, then the paces are increased the same amount on every right angle turn. This moves you out from your point of beginning, continually expanding your area.

Obviously, the walking of a square pattern will not begin until you have an assumed position that in your judgment is the closest to where you believe the camp might possibly be. Most often in the process of walking the squares, some familiar geographical fea-

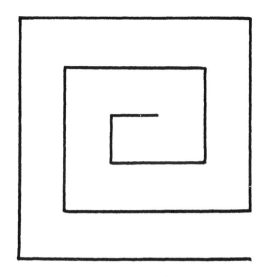

FIG. 38 *Pattern to Walk in Finding Camp*

ture is suddenly discovered and you know at once which direction from the recognized feature the camp is located.

Do not attempt to walk circles instead of squares. Circles cannot be systematically maintained.

There might be a tendency when night comes on to complete the squares by starlight and by compass or otherwise to make some rash effort to reach camp. This is a risk that generally should not be taken. An accidental fall into a declivity or over a precipice could reduce the chances of ever reaching camp to zero. Better to stop and wait for daylight. If the time is winter and one is properly dressed, the danger of freezing to death is rather remote unless the mistake is made of thrashing around until great fatigue causes a general functional depression. If there is no fuel for a fire, find a place to sit and just nap. You are not likely to freeze to death in your sleep, as is commonly believed. The increasing chill of your body will wake you, and by jumping around you will create enough warmth for another nap, enabling you to repeat this through the night. When morning comes, continue walking the square pattern. Arrival at camp and a good breakfast will relegate the ordeal of being lost to the limbo of forgotten events.*

* For comprehensive information on winter survival methods and travel, see my book *The New Way of the Wilderness,* published by The Macmillan Company.

CHAPTER SEVEN

Lines of Position

BEFORE aerial mapping cleared up many geographical mysteries of wilderness land and water, travel in wild regions with only a compass and the best existing maps often resulted in a complex guessing game. Somewhere in the confusion of islands, points, and bays of a hundred-mile lake, for example, was the outlet of a river, a portage trail, or a Hudson's Bay post. But where?

Many rivers were known only for a short distance inland from their mouths on the sea; from then on they were indicated on the map by conjectural, dotted lines trailing off into blank areas. Unless one used the trial-and-error method of travel into an unknown region, or could find an Indian, Eskimo, or other native who knew a part of the route by intimate association, travel became an adventurous exploration gamble.

In those earlier days I looked with the deepest admiration on such people as civil engineers and surveyors who could fix their exact positions anywhere by making transit or sextant sights on the sun, a star, or any other body in the sky.

By a stroke of good fortune, early one fall I entered the wilderness with an ex-Navy man who had navigated ships pretty much over the seven seas. Weeks later we were encamped upon a rock ledge of Canada's Pre-Cambrian Shield, several hundred miles from the rail head. Below lay a large, irregular, magnificent body of water that did not even appear on the map. Thousands of such lakes spread inviolate over Canada, connected by rivers and cascades—not dignified by so much as a name or, in many instances, even the conjectural, vague, dotted outline on a map.

At that juncture of our trip, we were not completely sure of our north-south position for access to the mouth of an unnamed river that was supposed to empty into the lake from the east. We had gained some mileage information about the location of the river's mouth earlier from the Indians. When darkness came on and we had discussed the uncertainty of how far north we needed to travel in order to reach the river's mouth, my companion opened a pack and brought out a small sextant and a separate artificial-horizon unit. The artificial horizon was basically nothing more than a pool of mercury, shielded from the wind by a collapsible glass housing. It is required on land to replace the natural horizon of the sea.

He waited until the Big Dipper assumed a particular position, then sighted his sextant on the Pole Star, fingering the index knob until the star and its reflected image in the mercury merged into a single unit. He read the result, divided this by 2, because the reflected image in the mercury had doubled the altitude. Then he handed the sextant to me.

I read the index on the sextant: 58 degrees, 13 minutes. "Now, what do I do?" I asked.

"Nothing. You've already done it," he replied.

"Done what?" I wanted to know.

"You have our latitude—our north-south position along this east shore. The altitude of the North Star above the horizon when the Dipper is in that position is the latitude," he explained.

It was that simple.

In order to fix the latitude line of position more precisely, a minor correction was needed; it was taken from the *Nautical Almanac*, read at a glance from a simple table on the inside cover. I found this a small matter. Soon, I was to make sextant sights for our position on Polaris every clear night, and also sights thereafter on the sun at noon for latitude. The sun sight required a few additional steps but these were relatively simple. With this knowledge the great vastness and complexity of Canada's wilderness began to unfold. It seemed less awesome, less intricate. Geographical factors started assuming their respective positions, heretofore having been strangely elusive, if not at times completely lost in a challenging maze of land and water.

There was some distance for me to go in the use of the sextant before I was to plot "fixes" for an exact position from both latitude and longitude, but I added knowledge each day and looked forward to pursuing at greater length this fascinating subject for the wilderness traveler. It took me some time to realize that the simple sight on Polaris or the sun for a latitude line of position alone was so great an advantage in the general route-finding program that if I acquired no more than this limited knowledge of the sextant's use, complemented by a compass, it could serve to guide me over most of the world's wilderness areas.

Many ships have traveled the oceans throughout the years, ships whose crews had no further knowledge of navigation than this simple sextant sight for latitude on the Pole Star, on Mintaka, or on the sun. There are captains of freighters today who manage to navigate their ships quite well with only this limited knowledge. If, for example, one were to leave New York and sail to Liverpool, it could be done simply by following an easterly course with a compass over the latitude line of position on which Liverpool is located—the latitude line maintained from time to time with a sextant by simple sights on such conveniently positioned bodies in the sky as the Pole Star, Mintaka, or the sun.

Again and again, we come back to that traditional, basic principle of route finding which we always need to bear in mind: the line of position. Ship captains who knew only how to make a sight for latitude headed over a compass line of position until they reached their required latitude line of position, then moved over the sea along this latitude line to port.

If, then, we can create a latitude line of position with an easy sextant sight on the sun, Polaris, or Mintaka (simple methods which are explained in Chapter 8), we always have a line of position on which to travel or to use as a base line over any wilderness land or water area. The latitude line of position—an east-west line—can, of course, be employed either as a short local line of position or as one encircling the world. (In all fairness here, I should interject that following a latitude line on a

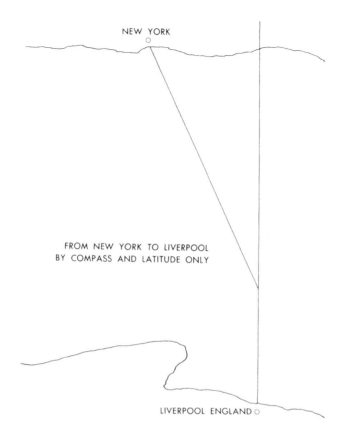

FIG. 39 *From New York to Liverpool by Compass and Latitude Line Only*

long sea voyage is not the shortest route between ports.)

If the reader examines any map, he sees that a latitude line (in fact, *any* line) drawn with a pencil across the map, will intersect many geographical fea-

tures such as rivers, railroads, lake shores, utility
roads, trails, and so on.

It will be clear at once that if we know how to
make a simple sextant sight for a latitude line of
position, we shall have not only a position line but
more particularly a fixed position wherever this latitude line crosses a natural or man-made base line.
The basic principle involved here in the intersection
of a latitude line of position with a natural or man-
made base line becomes an extremely valuable part
of our entire route-finding program.

The more nearly at right angles the latitude line

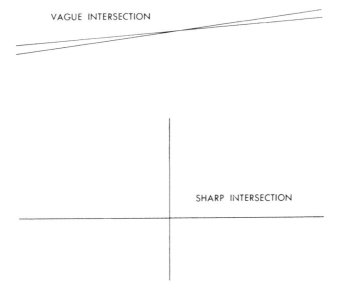

FIG. 40   *Sharp Intersection—Hazy Intersection*

FIG. 41   *Latitude Line of Position on River Bend*

crosses these various natural or man-made base lines, or coordinates as they are called, the more precise our fixed intersecting position points will be. But even when the latitude line forms a hazy intersection with the various base lines, or even if the latitude line fails entirely to form an actual intersection, much can be learned about one's own position by the mere proximity of a latitude line to a natural feature.

For example, we know that while traveling along a river, certain bends, falls, rapids, narrows, or lake-expansions occur, and while many such geographical features may be much alike, we are often able to identify them—and incidentally our own relative position on the river—merely by noting on the map how far the particular feature should be situated north or south from a recently shot latitude line.

In other words, the map will show the relation of

the feature to latitude. If the sextant-shot latitude corresponds to the map's latitude, the position of the feature will generally be apparent.

The nearness north or south of such a feature to a latitude line of position can thus on occasion prove almost as significant a combination for designating a position as a latitude line of position that actually intersects a particular feature.

This deductive reasoning regarding natural features as they relate to a latitude line of position or to a compass line of position applies to every kind of route-finding technique. The degree to which we apply this deductive ability can determine our success or failure as route finders. Route finding has often been said to be, and I think correctly so, as much an art as an exact science.

We can draw a fairly good example of the deductive process in position finding by studying Figure 41. The sketch shows that various characteristics of the river, its particular bends, rapids, narrows, etc., are identified not only by an actual intersection but also by the relative proximity of these features to the latitude line of position.

When we make a sextant sight for latitude, it is well, of course, for identification and comparison purposes to do so at a place that is a rather pronounced identifying feature in the river. This can be an abnormally wide or narrow part, a rapid or falls, or, best of all, at a bend in the river that will, if possible, allow the latitude line actually to intersect a particular feature in the river itself. Generally, after a little careful deduction, we can compare the features on the map with the actual ones by a combination of three factors: the relationship of the exact distance of the features from our latitude line of position; whether or not the features are north or south from the latitude line; and, probably more significant, the exact directional position in which the features lie. The law of probability is not apt to repeat these three exact circumstances in detail elsewhere.

It goes without saying that where the direction of a river lies north and south, or only roughly so, a latitude line will always cross the river and designate an exact point of position.

This route-finding process of relating the position of geographical features to latitude lines, of course, can apply to a variety of situations—not just to a river. A latitude line of position sighted with a sextant at the end of a certain bay or near some unusual configuration of a lake shoreline, for example, will give a position. Even the position of the latitude line as it parallels a segment of straight lake shore, may well fix a position—if we note the length of such a parallel.

The principle stated here obviously can apply in the same manner to other natural formations, such as coastlines, arroyos, mesas, mountain peaks, eskers, bench lands, and so forth.

In Chapter 5 we took into consideration the value of triangulation lines of position. If, now, we consider *a compass line of position sighted from a distant mountain peak or other geographical point* as it might *intersect a latitude line of position,* we have another extremely valuable combination of two different, artificially created position lines fixing an exact position in even an uncharted wilderness area (see Fig. 42).

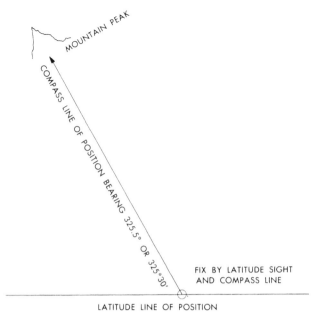

MOUNTAIN PEAK

COMPASS LINE OF POSITION BEARING 325.5° OR 325°30'

FIX BY LATITUDE SIGHT
AND COMPASS LINE

LATITUDE LINE OF POSITION

FIG. 42   *Fixing a Point by Latitude and Compass Lines
of Position*

A compass line of position sighted to a visible
distant point and intersecting a latitude line is a combination of factors exceptionally valuable near moun-
tainous country or on prairie, tundra, sea ice, or
desert where mountain peaks, identified or otherwise, are visible above the horizon at great or lesser
distances. The combination is also valuable on the
shore or even out on the surface of large bodies of
water where distant, identified islands, headlands, and
mountain peaks can be seen on the lake or in the
distance above the horizon.

The method for using this combination is, with a
compass having a good sighting device or with a

compact explorer's transit, to make a sight from our own position to a mountain peak, island, or headland. This sighted compass line is then laid down on the map with a protractor and a finely pointed pencil as an actual line of position. It will be seen that since a latitude line is always an east and west line, the distant mountain peak or other object sighted with a compass for a position line should, in order to intersect the latitude line, be one running more or less north and south from the observer. The more acute the compass line is to our latitude line, the sharper will be the *cut* at the intersection—thus more precisely pinpointing a position (see Fig. 42). I hasten to add, however, that any intersection of a compass line of position and a latitude line, regardless of how hazy, will have some value in fixing our position.

Once we have established a compass line of position by having sighted to a distant point, we proceed to make a sextant sight on the Pole Star, the star Mintaka, or the sun for a latitude line of position. This latitude line, which is a true east-west line, is then drawn across the map with the straight side of our protractor. The point of intersection of the two lines is our fixed position.

Since the latitude line of position, as will be shown in Chapter 8, is an easy and accurate one to determine, emphasis should always be placed on its use wherever it can intersect a compass line sighted to a mountain peak, island, or other helpful geographical point. This combination of latitude line and compass line provides a speedy and unique means of fixing a wilderness position—often replacing the working of a more involved astronomical problem ordinarily required in fixing a position by latitude and longitude.

When we make a sextant sight for latitude, we should not only make a record of the sextant sight in a diary, but also note the duration of travel over a given distance to or from this latitude line of position, along with a description of related, identifiable, geographical features within the visual area of our position on this latitude line. Such a record can be termed a travel log. I have found it best to include the date, hour, and minute when sights are made; the compass direction of travel; and any other incidental descriptive data available at the moment or place. A simple pencil sketch showing these factors adds graphically to the record. This travel log becomes valuable route-finding material. Then, we shall know by time and related factors not only the relation of landmarks to "something else" on the back trail or ahead, but also approximately when by our travel schedule we should have passed these landmarks or when we should reach them again on the return journey. Duration of travel from one latitude line or compass line of position to another gives a great deal of positive travel information when other complementary factors are considered along with duration of travel.

I like to regard the sextant-made latitude line or a compass line of position sighted on a known, distant, geographically fixed point as an actual trail leading over a stretch of wild country. The wilderness traveler who identifies his base camp or other objective as situated on a latitude line of position or a compass

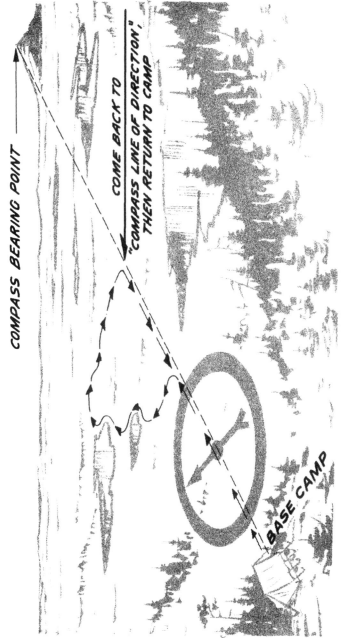

COMPASS BEARING POINT →

COME BACK TO
"COMPASS LINE OF DIRECTION",
THEN RETURN TO CAMP

BASE CAMP

FIG. 42. Compass Line Becomes Trail to Base Camp or Other Objective

line of position determined by a distant, visible, geographical feature truly has such a "trail."

Remember also that while latitude lines of position run only east-west, compass lines of position sighted to distant objectives can be not only east-west and north-south, but all 360 degree directions of the compass and may intersect the latitude line of position at most of the compass angles.

While the subject of navigation in its more conventional and general treatment can become involved, it is our good fortune in this short treatment of the subject that there are three unique and simple circumstances in navigation that allow us to make extremely easy and simple latitude sights with a sextant, without basic knowledge of navigation principles. These include the position of the Pole Star near the true pole, the almost-on-the-equator position of the star Mintaka when it is on our meridian, and the position of the sun when it is on our meridian at noon.

These three sights will be considered in easy ways to find the latitude of a place, as will be a simplified method for obtaining longitude. A short method for finding longitude is given here only for that occasion when circumstances do not permit intersecting a compass line of position with a latitude line of position. However, I cannot emphasize too much the value of avoiding the time-consuming longitude sight in the stress of travel whenever possible by using only the easily sighted latitude line of position to complement the natural intersecting geographical lines and the compass lines of position so far described. This simpler plan can uniquely expedite route finding for most.

It should also be explained here that longitude can be more accurately obtained by the longer conventional methods, such as H.O. 214, than by the short meridian-time sight given in the next chapter. This is because, in spite of the simplicity contained in the short method given herein, the need for determining to the exact second when the sun is on our meridian and the waiting interval required to complete the sight makes the process too uncertain and precarious under stress of travel.

H.O. 214 and other orthodox methods for obtaining longitude are too long to be considered in this simplified volume except the brief description of H.O. 214 given in the Appendix. The meridian-time sight, which is easy to understand, will work if used with care. The latitude sight, on the other hand, is exceptionally simple and certain in its accuracy because it does not require accurate time. For this reason, in an expedient route-finding program of very limited study, the latitude sight by its remarkable convenience becomes a boon to the average route finder. When no other north-south line of position except the time-arc longitude method is available to complement the latitude line of position, a radio line of position, described in Chapter 5, can be used to fix an exact position.

CHAPTER EIGHT

Route Finders in the Sky

DETERMINING LATITUDE AND LONGITUDE

A SIMPLE sextant sight on the Pole Star when it is east or west of the true pole will give an immediate latitude reading on the sextant without calculations of any kind.

Fortunately, we have an easy way of knowing when the Pole Star is approximately in these positions. The positions occur when the star Alkaid—the trailing star in the handle of the Big Dipper—is east or west from the Pole Star; that is, in an almost horizontal position with it, as shown in Figure 44.

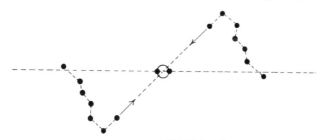

WHEN THE BIG DIPPER IS IN EITHER OF THESE POSITIONS THE CORRECTED ALTITUDE OF POLARIS IS EQUAL TO THE LATITUDE OF THE OBSERVER

FIG. 44 *Two Positions of Polaris for Latitude Sights*

A minor correction obtained at a glance from a table on the inside cover of the *Nautical Almanac* and merely subtracted from the sextant altitude of the star will give our *true* latitude.*

Example of Pole Star Sextant Sight

Altitude reading of the Pole Star on our sextant	55°	15.0'
Altitude correction taken from the inside cover of the *Nautical Almanac*	—	.7'
Our latitude	55°	14.3'

Latitude is shown in degrees and minutes along the margin of maps (60 minutes comprise a degree). Degrees and minutes are generally indicated by the following symbols:

degree   °
minute   ′

With this simple sextant sight on the Pole Star, available to everybody and requiring no special knowledge to obtain, we have a very important line of position that can apply basically to a great deal of our route finding.

For further simple methods of finding our latitude from a sextant sight on the Pole Star when the star is directly above or directly below the true pole and for a still further method of finding latitude from

* The *Nautical Almanac,* issued for each current year, is available from the Superintendent of Documents, U.S. Government Printing Office, Washington, D. C., 20402, for $3.50.

a sextant sight at any time of night, as well as for finding latitude from stars south of the equator, see the Appendix, pages 174-180.

There are various kinds of sextants in use, but they all do much the same thing—measure the height of a star or other body above the natural horizon or a horizon determined by a built-in level or a separate artificial-horizon unit. Continued use of the sextant gives added skill, of course, but no special knowledge is needed for its operation. The instrument is pointed at a star and the index knob turned until the star is seen in conjunction with one or the other of various horizons—artificial or natural.

In using the bubble sextant, with its built-in, artificial horizon, the index knob is turned until the sun (or star) appears to be in the center of the bubble. When the mercury-pool artificial horizon is used, the sextant is pointed at the sun (or star) reflected in the mercury pool and the index knob then turned until the actual sun and the reflected sun (or star) appear to merge into one. When the natural horizon is used, the index knob is turned until the sun (or star) appears in the sextant just to touch the horizon. The sextant altitude of the body in each of the three instances can then be read off at once on the sextant index.

While the bubble sextant with its built-in horizon level is principally designed for air navigation, the instrument can be readily adapted to stationary use on land, as shown in the above applications. A great many of these bubble sextants used by the Air Force are now available as government surplus from specialized dealers in scientific instruments.

Accuracy of the bubble sextant can be increased

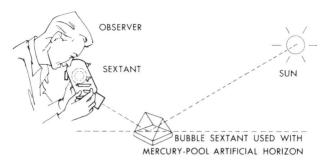

OBSERVER

SEXTANT

SUN

BUBBLE SEXTANT USED WITH
MERCURY-POOL ARTIFICIAL HORIZON

FIG. 45 *Bubble Sextant Used with Mercury-Pool Artificial Horizon*

when making the sight on land if it is supported on
a steady base or tripod. Any improvised, saddlelike
support will do. The bubble sextant is so constructed
with a reflecting prism and lens assembly that the
horizon bubble formed in the liquid when seen during a sight on a body in the sky resembles a tiny
doughnut suspended on its side in mid-air. When the
star or sun is fixed in the center of the bubble
(artificial horizon) by turning the sextant index
knob, you can at once read off the altitude of the
body on the index scale.

With a few twists of another knob while tipping
the bubble sextant on end, the bubble can be elimi-
nated, leaving a clear field for use with the sea
horizon or for use with a separate artificial-horizon
unit. A few more twists of the same knob while holding the sextant level will again re-form a bubble for
land or plane-flight use.

When making a sextant sight on land, still greater
accuracy than the bubble artificial horizon allows
can be had by eliminating the bubble, as described,
and using the sextant with a separate, artificial-

horizon unit. The horizon unit can be an auxiliary precision level attached to the sextant and adjusted with capstan-type screws. (See Fig. 46A.) The most accurate type, though not as convenient as the level, consists of little more than a small pool of mercury in a nonmetal basin (wood or glass) set inside a wedge-shaped, glass housing (using optically flat or perfect sheet glass), so that the wind will not disturb the surface of the mercury. The horizon unit can easily be constructed as a do-it-yourself project at home as shown in Figure 46B.

FIG. 46A   *Bubble Sextant Provided with Sensitive Auxiliary Level*

FIG. 46B *Mercury-Pool Artificial-Horizon Unit*

When the elevation of a body above the horizon
is measured with a sextant using the mercury-pool
artificial horizon, the altitude becomes doubled by
reflection in the mercury—the body in the sextant ap-
pearing to be both above and below the horizon.
Only half of this doubled sextant reading, of course,
is used to obtain the sextant altitude of the body,
then the minor correction from the *Nautical Almanac*

table is applied, as previously explained, to obtain the true altitude.

The standard marine sextant with either vernier-

FIG. 47A *Marine Sextant with Vernier-Type Reading*

or micrometer drum-type reading can also be used on land with the above-described mercury artificial-horizon unit. Artificial-horizon units of the mercury-pool type cannot be used at sea or on other large bodies of water because the mercury is disturbed by the movement of the ship or other craft. Either the bubble sextant using the bubble or natural horizon or the marine sextant using the natural horizon can be employed for such sights. However, in wilderness canoe travel, one can usually go ashore, where the mercury artificial horizon or auxiliary level horizon can be set up on solid ground for a precise sight. The bubble sextant has been used at sea when the natural horizon was not distinct, but the natural horizon when it can be seen is much preferred.

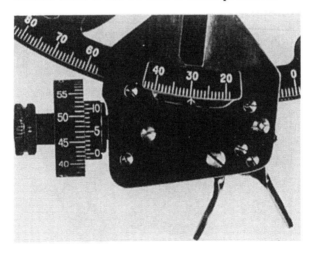

FIG. 47B *Micrometer Drum-Type Reading Assembly Only of Marine Sextant*

FIG. 47C *Sun Tangent with Natural Horizon As Seen in Marine Sextant*

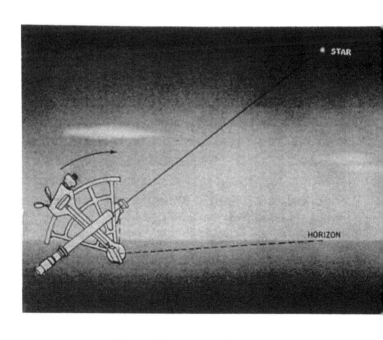

FIG. 47D *Marine Sextant Used Upside-Down When Horizon Is in Weak Contrast*

The standard marine sextant, when used in its common position, will bring the celestial body down to the horizon as shown in Figure 47C. Where a poor contrast is had between sky and sea horizon the sextant is sometimes used upside-down as in Figure 47D.

On expeditions where all route-finding observations can be made on land or ice, a compact explorer's transit, or theodolite, secured on a tripod, is more convenient for all-around work than a sextant. The transit, or theodolite, besides having its own built-in level (artificial horizon) for altitude sights on the sun and stars, has an added advantage: its precision-sighting scope can also be used in triangulation work, such as fixing one's position with lines of position sighted to islands, points, mountain peaks, and so forth, as described in Chapter 7. Where travel is by plane, the bubble sextant, of course, is used; and if travel is entirely on bodies of water large enough for seeing a natural horizon, a standard marine-type sextant is the choice. However, when a plane can be set down on water near shore or on ice, a transit can be set up on the shore or on the ice to great advantage for measuring altitude, for triangulation, and for other special uses.

A so-called pocket transit, patterned after the original Brunton design and now marketed by several instrument firms, deserves consideration here because of its unique and versatile features. The unit, $3'' \times 3'' \times 1''$ in size and weighing only 8 ounces, is readily carried in the pocket. It has a precision-made compass with a luminous needle. The compass can be had either with a 0-to-360-degree counterclockwise dial or with quadrant calibrations (see Appendix, Quadrant Calibration, pages 197-199). Its equip-

FIG. 48A *Mountain or Explorer's Transit*

FIG. 48B *Light, Compact, Explorer's Theodolite*

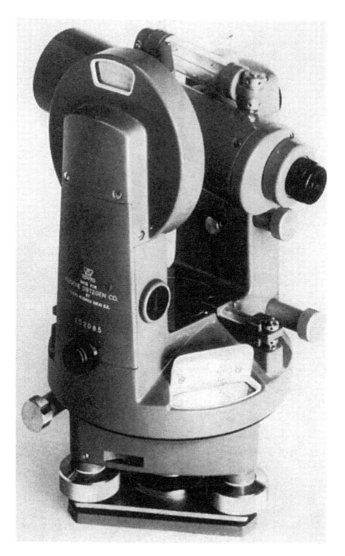

FIG. 48C *"Top-Site" Transit*

FIG. 49   *Pocket Transit*

ment for sighting compass bearings is a long, swing-out bar with both peep sights and open sights. The cover has a split-view mirror with a lubber's line in the center, so one can read the compass dial and sight on a distant objective point at the same time. With the aid of the mirror a back sight on the trail can also be made to align with a forward point on the trail.

The transit assembly of this unit is provided with a vernier (an adapter scale for reading parts of divisions) which permits reading to 5 minutes of arc. The taking of a number of sights on the same star or the sun might give an average closer than 5 minutes. An instrument with so broad a reading cannot wholly replace a standard transit or sextant, but it does provide a handy complement unit for each member of an exploration party where a high-precision transit or sextant is also carried.

Since the pocket transit comes equipped with an aluminum, telescopic tripod, some advantage in weight saving can also be had by adapting the tripod as a camera support. An adapter bushing would be required for this. The pocket transit costs about $50. Whenever weight of equipment becomes a factor this tripod convertibility should be applied to all additional instruments requiring support, such as sextants, theodolites, compasses, etc.

LATITUDE LINE OF POSITION FROM THE NOONDAY SUN

A latitude line of position can also be had by a simple sextant sight on the sun at high noon, when it crosses our meridian, without the need for accurate time and only with the added knowledge of the sun's declination—that is, the sun's latitude along the earth. Declination is readily obtained from the *Nautical Almanac*.

It is vitally important in our route-finding observations that we regard the sun as moving along the earth's surface throughout the day from east to west and seasonally from north to south and south to north. When we think of the sun as moving along the earth's surface in this fashion, our problem becomes much simpler. The *Nautical Almanac*, which gives the position of the sun on the earth for every second in the year, is based on this premise—that the sun is moving along the earth's surface.

Thus, when we refer to the position of three factors—the equator, the sun, and our own position—we need to think of all three as having an earth-surface position, or as moving along the earth's surface.

In the example to follow, when the sun's earth-surface position is between our position and the equator, our latitude is equal to 90 degrees minus the corrected altitude of the sun, plus the declination (or latitude) of the sun. Let us examine this simple observation in detail.

Since the sun has a particular position along the earth surface north or south of the equator for each moment of the year, if we can determine our own distance north or south from the sun's position, we should have no trouble, as we shall see, in finding our distance north or south from the equator—this distance from the equator being our latitude.

While the sun's apparent, daily movement across

the earth from east to west is rapid, it so happens that the sun's continual, hourly movement north or south from the equator along the earth surface throughout the year is slow. For this reason, if the sun's earth-surface position, that is, its latitude or declination north or south of the equator in degrees and minutes, is taken from the *Nautical Almanac* at only the *approximate* time of making the sextant sight, no appreciable error will occur in a sextant-sighted latitude line of position. Due to this fortunate, slow movement of the sun north and south over the earth surface, our sight on the sun for latitude, as we shall see, becomes extremely convenient and easy to complete.

When looking through a sextant sighted on the sun and using the mercury artificial horizon, two sun images appear: the direct sun and the sun's reflected image in the mercury. The dark-glass sun shields supplied on the sextant, when brought into position, show the true sun and the reflected sun in the mercury as clearly defined green disks. For an altitude reading of the sun, the index need only be turned until both green disks merge into one. This merging of the two sharply defined disks gives a clear, convenient, and very accurate sighting arrangement. Remember that because of the double image only one-half the altitude reading is used for finding the latitude.

Procedure

To make our example for finding latitude more realistic and clear, let us assume that we are traveling along the west coast of Hudson Bay in Canada—

that we are trying to find the mouth of the Thlewiaza River, one of many rivers that empty into the bay. From our map we have already learned the position of the river's mouth itself to be approximately 60 degrees, 25 minutes north latitude. Our own position on the coast is unknown. Required: the latitude of our position, so that we will know which direction and how far we need to travel north or south along the coast to reach the river's mouth.

With a compass we roughly determine when the sun, in its travel east to west over the earth surface, will be nearing our own meridian—our meridian being a true north-south line directly across our own position. The sextant reading of the sun at high noon is what we are looking for to complete our example.

In order not to miss the time when this highest reading takes place, we start making sextant sights of the sun shortly before the sun crosses our meridian so that we do not miss the approximate time when it crosses. We continue making such sights at about one-minute intervals until the sun reaches its highest elevation above the horizon at our position and begins its downward path shortly after the high point of noon. For our use we now select the highest altitude reading from those we have taken. (There will be several of the highest altitudes at high noon that are the same, because the sun when on the meridian sort of "hangs" for a few minutes at the same altitude.)

When we have made this single selection from the highest meridian altitudes of the sun, we subtract the correction for this particular altitude, taken from the inside front cover of the *Nautical Almanac,*

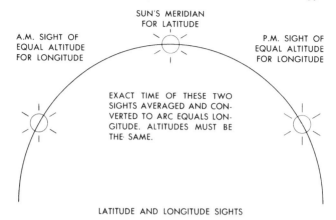

SUN'S MERIDIAN
FOR LATITUDE

A.M. SIGHT OF
EQUAL ALTITUDE
FOR LONGITUDE

P.M. SIGHT OF
EQUAL ALTITUDE
FOR LONGITUDE

EXACT TIME OF THESE TWO
SIGHTS AVERAGED AND CON-
VERTED TO ARC EQUALS LON-
GITUDE. ALTITUDES MUST BE
THE SAME.

LATITUDE AND LONGITUDE SIGHTS

FIG. 50   *Latitude and Longitude Sights*

the same as we did for the Pole Star, treated earlier
in this chapter. When this correction is applied to the
sextant altitude, it is called the corrected altitude.
(For simplicity, when sights of the sun are made on
land with a bubble sextant or when using the
mercury-pool horizon, we can use the same altitude
correction table for the sun as given on the inside
cover of the *Nautical Almanac* for stars.)

Since our position on the shore of Hudson Bay is
north of the equator, let us assume in our example
that the sun, in moving along the earth surface, is
now north of the equator at the time we make our
sextant sight—which in fact it would be, say, in
August.

Our next step is to determine how far north of
the sun's position on the earth surface our own position happens to be. If we can do this—and we can,
by the simplest arithmetic, as we shall see—all we

need do in order to find our latitude is to add the
sun's distance north of the equator (its declination)
to our own distance from the sun (zenith distance).
This simple addition will give our own distance from
the equator, which is our latitude. Each step will
presently be followed out.

Steps Required

Note in the accompanying illustration that the
horizontal line is our own horizon. The vertical line
is our own overhead position, or zenith, as it is
called. These two lines form a 90-degree, or right,
angle.

Since adding or subtracting angles is just simple
arithmetic, if we now merely subtract our corrected
sextant altitude of the sun at high noon in degrees
and minutes from the 90-degree angle, we immediately have the distance between our own position
on the earth surface and the sun's position along
the earth surface in degrees and minutes. The distance from our own earth-surface position to the
sun's earth-surface position is called the zenith distance. If the 90-degree-angle illustration is again
carefully observed, the subtraction of our altitude
from 90 degrees to obtain zenith distance is easily
followed. In our particular example on Hudson Bay,
all we need do now is add these degrees and minutes
of zenith distance to the declination (latitude) of the
sun in degrees and minutes, as we shall presently do.
The result will be our latitude.

In assuming our position to be on the west coast of
Hudson Bay, we don't have to be concerned about
our longitude because we can look on the map and

check this at the point where our own sighted line of position crosses the coastline. The coastline latitude as shown on the map will, of course, be our longitude.

By subtracting our own latitude in degrees and minutes from the latitude of the river's mouth in degrees and minutes, taken from the map, we have the difference in latitude of the two positions—the river's mouth and our position—in degrees and minutes.

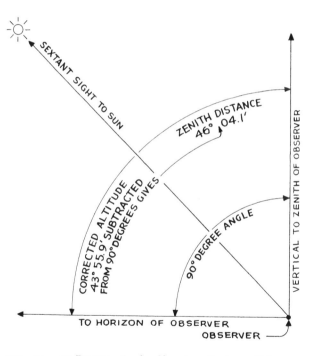

FIG. 51 *90-Degree Angle Showing Sextant Sight on Sun for Latitude*

We can readily convert these degrees and minutes of latitude into miles. There are 60 nautical miles in 1 degree of latitude. A convenient rule to remember for converting nautical miles into statute miles is that 6.6 nautical miles equal 7.6 statute or regular miles, so that on this basis we can easily estimate in round figures our distance to the river's mouth.

To sum up, then, we have the following easy steps for obtaining a latitude line of position by a sextant sight of the sun at the shore of Hudson Bay when the sun's position on the earth surface and our own position are north of the equator:

1. Measure the altitude of the sun with a sextant or transit at high noon, taking several sights and selecting only one—the highest.

2. Subtract the correction for this altitude, using the star table on the inside front cover of the *Nautical Almanac* if a bubble sextant or an artificial horizon is used. This gives the corrected altitude.

   If the natural horizon of Hudson Bay is used, apply the sun-table correction on the inside cover of the *Nautical Almanac* instead of the star table. (See Altitude Corrections, pages 190-191, in Appendix for the natural-horizon method.)

3. Subtract the measured, corrected sextant altitude of the sun from 90 degrees (see illustration). This gives the zenith distance (the distance of our own earth-surface position from the sun's earth-surface position).

4. From the table in the daily pages of the *Nautical Almanac* for the proper date, find the declination of the sun for approximate noon only.

5. Add the zenith distance in degrees and minutes, to the declination of the sun in degrees and minutes.

6. The result is our latitude line of position in degrees and minutes.

Example

Measured sextant altitude	43°	56.9'
Correction from inside cover of the *Nautical Almanac*	—	01.0'
Corrected altitude	43°	55.9'
Horizon to zenith as in the 90°-angle sketch	90°	00'
Corrected altitude	—43°	55.9'
Zenith distance	46°	04.1'
Declination (latitude) of sun at high noon taken from the *Nautical Almanac* (daily page)	+13°	15.1'
Our latitude on the shore of Hudson Bay	59°	19.2'
Latitude of Thlewiaza River taken from the map	60°	25'
Our own latitude on Hudson Bay	—59°	19.2'
Difference in latitude between our own position on Hudson Bay and the Thlewiaza River	01°	05.8'
Or, converted to minutes of arc		65.8'

Since 1 minute of latitude is equal to 1 nautical

mile, 65.8 minutes of latitude equal 65.8 nautical miles, or when converted to statute miles, approximately 75 miles—the difference in statute miles between our position on Hudson Bay and the mouth of the Thlewiaza River, yet to be traveled on our journey up the coast.

Because the data in the *Nautical Almanac* changes each year, the figures used in the foregoing example

LONGITUDE AND COAST

MAINLAND

LATITUDE OF
THLEWIAZA RIVER
MOUTH 60°25′

MAINLAND

HUDSON BAY

TO RIVER 75 MILES

OUR POSITION ON HUDSON BAY
59°19.2′

FIG. 52   *Showing Relative Distance between Thlewiaza River and Point of Observation*

are arbitrarily taken at random. In working an example of his own, the reader will, of course, apply data from the latest *Almanac*.

In the example given for finding our latitude from the noonday sun, 90 degrees minus our corrected altitude, plus the declination of the sun, became our latitude.

There are, of course, other positions of the sun in combination with our own position north and south of the equator to consider. Basically the problem is much the same. These are given and diagramed in the following:

When the equator is between our earth-surface position and the sun's earth-surface position, our latitude is determined by 90 degrees minus corrected altitude, minus declination of the sun.

When our earth-surface position is between the sun's earth-surface position and the equator, our latitude equals declination of the sun, minus zenith distance. (Zenith distance equals 90 degrees minus corrected altitude.)

FINDING OUR LONGITUDE

We have already seen how we can determine our latitude by a combination of rather simple sextant sights on the sun at high noon. If we utilize somewhat the same combination of sextant sights for the sole purpose of determining when the sun is exactly on our own meridian, we can also determine our longitude from this. The main point to remember is that *when the sun at noon is centered exactly on our particular meridian, the sun's longitude*

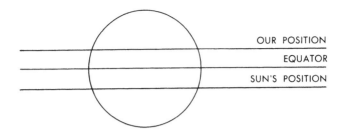

FIG. 53 *Our Position—Equator—Sun's Position*

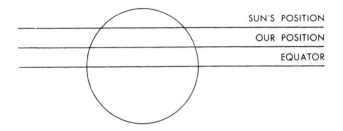

FIG. 54 *Sun's Position—Our Position—Equator*

along the earth's surface is the same as our own. It goes without saying that if we can learn the sun's longitude when it is on our own meridian, we will at once have our own longitude. In other words, a north-and-south longitude line drawn through our own position would also pass through the sun's earth-surface position at high noon.

Unlike our latitude sight, which did not require exact time, we must in obtaining longitude have the *exact time to the second* in order to determine the moment when the sun crosses our meridian. A 24-hour dial watch set to exact Greenwich Mean Time is needed for this, or we can convert regular zone watch time to Greenwich Mean Time (see page 183 in

Appendix for this conversion). The time obtained from government time signals with a small, portable radio, is the most dependable method of providing exact time. The best watch cannot maintain accurate time to an exact second very long. The United States broadcasts Eastern Standard Time over short-wave every 5 minutes, Canada every minute throughout the 24 hours. This will have to be converted to Greenwich Mean Time.

PROCEDURE FOR FINDING OUR LONGITUDE

Approximately 20 minutes *before* the sun reaches its highest noontime altitude, take a series of five or more sextant sights on the sun at about half minute intervals. Follow this with another series of five or more sights at half minute intervals about 20 minutes *after* the sun's highest noontime altitude. Sights should be taken in both A.M. and P.M. series as frequently as possible with leisure and accuracy, although half minute intervals usually suffice. If the two series of sights are taken in spans of time more than 20 minutes before and more than 20 minutes after the sun crosses our meridian, the accuracy of the longitude sight will increase. In other words, if we can get a series of sights when the sun is most rapidly climbing toward noon and a series when the sun is most rapidly dropping from noon, rather than when the sun is beginning to level off at noon, accuracy is improved (see Fig. 55).

No time need be lost on the trail between the A.M. and P.M. series of sextant sights, because the noontime lunch period can consume the interval.

The *altitude* of each sight taken, along with its

exact second of time, must be systematically recorded, preferably in a notebook. If one member of
the party makes the sextant sights while a second
member keeps time and records the instant of each
sight, the operation is smoother. A stopwatch is
necessary if a person is working alone.

After making the series of A.M. and P.M. altitude
sights, select a single altitude reading from those
taken before the sun reached high noon that will correspond with an altitude taken after the sun reached
high noon, *noting the exact moments of time* when
each of these two A.M. and P.M. sights were taken.

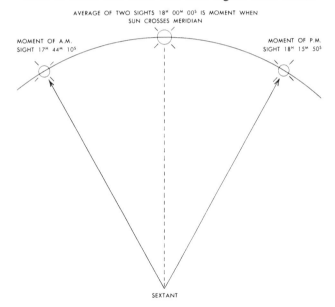

FIG. 55   *Noontime Arc of Sun with Equal Altitudes for
Determining Longitude*

Add the two *times* of making the sights (not the altitudes) and divide the result by two. The average, or mean, of the two times will be the exact moment of time when the sun crossed the meridian. This mean time, converted to degrees, minutes, and seconds of arc using the conversion table in the *Nautical Almanac,* will be our longitude. Or consider that

I hour of time	= 15 degrees of longitude
I minute of time	= 15 minutes of longitude
I second of time	= 15 seconds of longitude

Example

Let us assume that the Greenwich Mean Time for the before-noon sight was 17 hours, 44 minutes, 10 seconds; the afternoon sight 18 hours, 15 minutes, 50 seconds. (Remember that 1 degree = 60 minutes of arc, 1 minute = 60 seconds of arc.)

A.M. sight	17h	44m	10s
P.M. sight	+18h	15m	50s
Total time of sights	36h	00m	00s
Divided by 2	=18h	00m	00s,

or the average of the two A.M. and P.M. times being the moment of time when the sun crossed the meridian.

Now, if we take this 18 hours of Greenwich Mean Time (GMT) and consult the *Nautical Almanac* for the date we made the sight, we will find listed in the

sun table the longitude of the sun, called Greenwich
Hour Angle (GHA), for this 18 hours of Greenwich
Mean Time. So, when we read off the longitude of
the sun's earth-surface position in the *Almanac* for
18 hours, we have our own longitude, which in this
example has been a west longitude. (Our position,
as you see, was west of the Greenwich Meridian;
west of 00 longitude.)

The foregoing example for obtaining our longitude
was purposely made to come out an even 18 hours
for ease in citing our example, so that we could go to
the *Nautical Almanac* with a round figure. But, of
course, this convenient round figure of time generally
does not occur.

The exact time of the sun's meridian transit might
have been at an uneven moment of time, say, 18
hours, 37 minutes, 12 seconds, or some other such
odd moment of time. What we do in a case of this
kind is first to look in the *Nautical Almanac* under
the date we made the sights and record the sun's
longitude (GHA) as we did for 18 hours. Then, by
going to the convenient table in the back yellow
pages of the *Nautical Almanac,* we would at a glance
find how far the sun has traveled during these extra
37 minutes and 12 seconds.

The *Almanac* table shows that the sun travels 9
degrees and 18 minutes of longitude in 37 minutes
and 12 seconds of time, so we simply add the 9
degrees and 18 minutes to the longitude for 18 hours
and we have the west longitude of the sun when
it transits our meridian. And again, since the sun's
longitude when it is on our meridian is the same as
our own, we also have our own longitude.

Example

Let us say that we are making a sight for west
longitude on a day in the year and at a place when
the sun crosses our meridian at the above time of
18 hours, 37 minutes, 12 seconds. In the daily sun
table of the *Nautical Almanac* we find the longitude
of the sun (GHA) at 18 hours for that day to be 92
degrees, 22.4 minutes. The table in the yellow pages
of the *Nautical Almanac* will show that the longitude
traveled by the sun in 37 minutes, 12 seconds is 9
degrees, 18 minutes—the total of these being 101
degrees, 40.4 minutes.

Longitude for 18 hours	92°	22.4'
For 37 minutes, 12 seconds	+ 09°	18.0'
For 18 hours, 37 minutes,		
12 seconds	101°	40.4'
	(our longitude)	

We thus have a longitude line of position. If we
also obtained a *latitude* line of position from an observation of the noon sun, as previously described,
the intersection of these two lines would be our exact
position, called a fix.

Wherever a longitude line is the only alternative
for intersecting a latitude line to fix a position, an
effort should first be made to substitute the longitude
line with a radio line of position described in Chapter 5. A radio line intersecting a latitude line will fix
a postion as well, and avoid taking the more involved
longitude sight.

APPENDIX

Contained in this appendix are several additional variations of simplified route-finding forms, along with general miscellany and a few glossary terms. The glossary and general data in this appendix are not given alphabetically but rather in a sequence best suited to complement the previous chapters and the increasing further interest of the reader. The writing of an appendix in a book on route finding becomes almost inevitable. How else does one escalate the reader's interest beyond the actual essentials, to prove that "a little knowledge is a dangerous thing"?

Perhaps books dealing with information should be written so that the reader can make an exit from the subject anywhere, taking his information in the degree he chooses. This book is written pretty much that way. You will recall, for example, that in Chapter 8 a sextant sight on Polaris gave the latitude immediately without further fuss or bother. Perhaps you say, "Why not stop there? Polaris is usually around on a clear night, why concern myself with the sun?" This occurred to me, too, when first I found that a sextant sight on Polaris would quickly do the job without calculation. But the gremlins of position finding are not, I found, that easy to escape. There was the sun looking down day after day with a bold challenge—"I dare you to try a sight on me!"

A continuing interest in route finding thus becomes as alluring as the call of the wild itself. The deeper into the wilderness one goes with this knowledge, the deeper one wants to go.

OTHER SIMPLE METHODS FOR FINDING LATITUDE

LATITUDE BY SEXTANT SIGHT ON POLARIS AT UPPER OR
LOWER CULMINATION (ABOVE OR BELOW THE POLE),
ALSO CALLED UPPER AND LOWER TRANSIT

In Chapter 8 a method was given for finding our latitude from the Pole Star when the star is directly east or directly west of the true pole, that is, when the Pole Star and the true elevated pole are in a horizontal position—what we call east or west elongation. This became the simplest method possible. But we can also find our latitude from the Pole Star when it is directly above or directly below the true pole—that is, in a vertical position with it. We call this upper or lower culmination. We can use this method without time or special navigation knowledge, as follows:

Procedure

We determine when the Pole Star is directly above or directly below the true pole by the position of the star Alkaid (the trailing star at the end of the Big Dipper's handle). In this present example, when the star Alkaid is *above* the Pole Star, that is, in an almost vertical position with it, as shown in Figure 20, the Pole Star is then directly below the true pole. It is plain to see that if with our sextant we measured the altitude of the Pole Star when the star was below the pole, since our altitude of the pole is equal to our latitude, we would merely have to add to our corrected altitude the distance from the Pole Star to the true pole (polar distance) to get our latitude.

In short, corrected sextant altitude of the Pole Star when it is directly below the true pole, plus polar distance, equals our latitude.

Polar-distance tables, contained in a booklet called *Solar Ephemeris Manual,* issued annually, can be obtained free from any surveying-instrument company. These tables give the polar distance by simple inspection for all times of the year and require no computation. Otherwise, polar distance is easily determined, since polar distance equals 90 degrees minus the declination of the star. (For declination of any celestial body by simple inspection, see the *Nautical Almanac.*)

On the other hand, when the Pole Star happens to be directly above the true pole, that is, when we find the star Alkaid *below* the Pole Star in an almost vertical position with it, as shown in Figure 20, all we need do is subtract the polar distance from the corrected sextant altitude and we have our latitude. (Remember that "corrected" sextant altitude is simply the sextant altitude with the refraction correction taken from the inside cover of the *Nautical Almanac* and applied as described in Chapter 8.)

POLAR DISTANCE

For those who wish to use a transit in finding an exact bearing from Polaris for some precise work in the field, the *Solar Ephemeris,* just mentioned, will give the polar distance of Polaris for all times of the year. The bearing of Polaris at elongation is thus given for each latitude up to 70°. Such bearings are accurate and should be used in preference to magnetic-compass bearings wherever high precision is required.

LATITUDE BY SEXTANT SIGHT ON THE POLE STAR AT
ANY TIME OF NIGHT, USING *Nautical Almanac*
POLE-STAR TABLES

With an annual copy of the *Nautical Almanac* on hand we have available to us a convenient and accurate method for making a sight on the Pole Star for a latitude line of position at any time of night.

Procedure

Correct Greenwich Mean Time is required for this sight. A sextant sight is made on Polaris and the altitude corrected for refraction, as we did in Chapter 8 (using the table inside the front cover of the *Nautical Almanac*). The *Nautical Almanac* is then entered with the exact Greenwich Mean Time of the sextant sight. On the left-hand side of the daily pages we find a column labeled Aries. (See definition of Aries in this appendix. For convenience here an understanding of the definition may be disregarded.) From the Aries column alongside the exact time of the sight, we take the Greenwich Hour Angle (GHA) of Aries. From this Greenwich Hour Angle of Aries, we now subtract our longitude if we are in west longitude or add our longitude if we are in east longitude in order to obtain the *local hour angle* of Aries. With this local-hour angle of Aries, we turn to the Pole Star tables in the back of the *Nautical Almanac*. There, listed under our local-hour angle, we find the three needed corrections that are to be applied to our corrected altitude, clearly and simply explained at the bottom of the page. These, corrections are labeled a_0, a_1, a_2 and can be read off at a glance without calculation. Latitude then will equal corrected sextant altitude, minus 1 degree, plus the a_0, a_1, a_2 corrections.

LATITUDE BY SEXTANT SIGHT ON MINTAKA (ORIONIS DELTA)

In the Southern Hemisphere we need a star conveniently located in the sky for finding latitude, because there the handy Pole Star cannot be seen. Of course, there are various stars south of the equator on which observations can be made for latitude; but in this concise field volume, we are selecting only those well-positioned stars so situated in the sky as to greatly simplify our observations.

The position of the star Mintaka happens to be another of those fortunate star-position circumstances where we can derive easy route-finding data without mathematical complications, because Mintaka is almost on the equator. A sextant sight of a celestial body on the equator when that body is also on our meridian creates a situation where our zenith distance (90 degrees minus corrected altitude) is equal to our latitude.

From the foregoing we can conclude that Mintaka is extremely valuable for finding latitude when Mintaka transits (crosses) our meridian. This is important because Mintaka is visible in both the Southern and Northern Hemisphere—except at the poles and during that time of year when Mintaka transits the meridian in the daytime and is invisible. In both hemispheres, unfortunately, this is half the year. We should bear in mind, however, that at certain times of the year, if Mintaka cannot be seen in the early part of the night, it might be seen in the hours before dawn.

Mintaka is easily found in the heavens by locating the constellation Orion and then noting the three stars in Orion's Belt. Mintaka is the one of these three belt stars farthest from Sirius, the Dog Star, the brightest in the sky. In star charts, Mintaka appears right on the equator because its distance south of the equator is too negligible to be shown graphically. Unfortunately, Mintaka is not listed in the *Nautical Almanac,* but the middle star in Orion's Belt, Alnilam, which is only 1 degree, 13 minutes from the equator, is listed and can be used in place of Mintaka, if desired, using the same following procedure as for Mintaka.

Procedure

Determine when Mintaka is closely nearing our north-south meridian line by a rough compass observation (see Meridian Passage in this appendix). Start taking sextant sights on Mintaka and continue taking them until the highest altitude is reached (as we did in Chapter 8 for the noonday sun, except that with

Mintaka, it will, of course, be an observation at night). Make the simple refraction correction taken from the star table on the inside cover of the *Nautical Almanac* described for the Pole Star in Chapter 8.

This highest correct altitude of Mintaka subtracted from 90 degrees, minus 20 minutes of arc when we are in the Northern Hemisphere, will be our latitude. More accurately, Mintaka in 1965 was 19 minutes, 24.97 seconds south of the equator and will be moving toward the equator at the rate of about 3 seconds of arc per year.

If the star Alnilam is used instead of Mintaka, the correction in the Northern Hemisphere will be minus 1 minute, 13 seconds; and in the Southern Hemisphere, plus 1 minute, 13 seconds. Check the declination of Alnilam annually in the *Nautical Almanac* and apply the correction accordingly.

Examples for Both Hemispheres

For Mintaka when our position is in	NORTHERN HEMISPHERE		
The angle between our horizon and zenith		90°	00′
Assume corrected altitude to be		— 28°	36′
Zenith distance		61°	24′
Northern Hemisphere Mintaka correction		—	20′
Our North latitude		61°	04′

For Mintaka when our position is in   SOUTHERN HEMISPHERE

The angle between our horizon and

zenith	90°	00′
Assume corrected altitude to be	— 29°	16′

Zenith distance	60°	44′
Southern Hemisphere Mintaka		
correction	+	20′

Our South latitude	61°	04′

If the star Alnilam, because of its inclusion in the *Nautical Almanac,* is used instead of Mintaka, our latitude will be: corrected altitude subtracted from 90 degrees, minus the declination of Alnilam when we are in the Northern Hemisphere or plus the declination when we are in the Southern Hemisphere—using the same method followed above for Mintaka. In the above subtraction, remember, 1° = 60′ not 100.

MERIDIAN PASSAGE

Meridian passage is the moment when the sun, a star, or another body transits (passes over) the meridian of the observer or some other indicated meridian of the earth, such as the Greenwich Meridian. In Chapter 8, you will recall, both latitude and longitude were determined by meridian transits of the sun. It may be noted here for the enterprising reader that latitude and longitude can also be found by a sextant sight of any star as it transits the meridian of the observer.

When a star is at upper transit, that is, passes over the observer's meridian above the pole, the same general procedure for a meridian sight to obtain latitude can be used as outlined for the sun, requiring only a corrected altitude and the star's declination. But we also have an opportunity in the higher latitudes for such sights when the star transits the lower meridian, that is, crosses our meridian below the pole. The following simple procedure can be used for this subpolar sight. Assume the star to be Kochab:

Latitude, then, equals corrected altitude of Kochab, plus its polar distance (polar distance is 90 degrees minus declination of the body).

Example

The angle between our horizon and		
zenith	90°	00′
Declination of Kochab	− 74°	18.3′
Polar distance of Kochab	15°	41.7′
Corrected altitude	+ 34°	30.3′
Our latitude	50°	12.0′

LEARNING THE MERIDIAN TRANSIT OF THE SUN FROM THE *Nautical Almanac*

If the *longitude,* and not the latitude, of our own position is known, the time when the sun transits our meridian can be determined for a latitude sight, without the labor of taking a series of sextant sights as suggested in Chapter 8.

Procedure

Open the *Nautical Almanac* to the proper date of making the sight. In the lower right-hand corner of the daily page, you will find the moment of time when the sun transits the meridian of Greenwich. From the Arc-to-Time Table in the back of the *Almanac,* convert your own longitude to time, or consider that

1 degree of longitude = 4 minutes of time
1 minute of longitude = 4 seconds of time
1 second of longitude = approximately .07
                                       seconds of time

This conversion of our longitude to time (arc to time) will give the amount of *time* it will take for the sun to travel from the Greenwich Meridian to our own meridian. In west longitude, by *adding* this time to the moment of time when the sun transits the Greenwich Meridian, we will have the exact time when the sun transits our own meridian. If we are in east longitude, we proceed as above, except that we *subtract* the time obtained from our converted longitude to obtain the sun's moment of transit over our meridian.

GREENWICH MEAN TIME

Greenwich Mean Time, a time used by navigators over the world, is the time at Greenwich, England, that a 24-hour watch reads when you make your sextant sight anywhere. Navigational watches, keeping Greenwich Mean Time, are highly accurate watches that read to 24 hours instead of 12 to avoid confusing one 12-hour period of the day with another. Greenwich Mean Time is abbreviated GMT. Accurate time, as stated earlier, can be had by short-wave radio.

VALUE OF HAVING GREENWICH MEAN TIME

Nautical Almanac tables are based on Greenwich Mean Time. While our problem of sighting the sun with a sextant at high noon is comparatively simple, it can be made even more so if we carry a watch having a 24-hour dial, set to Greenwich Mean Time. As indicated earlier, the exact time is really not needed for a latitude-meridian sight of the sun, but the convenience of having Greenwich Mean Time helps us learn approximately when to make the sight. With a Greenwich Mean Time watch, we can also more readily read off the sun's declination from the sun table in the *Nautical Almanac*. (See Latitude Line of Position from the Noonday Sun, in Chapter 8.)

CONVERTING GREENWICH MEAN TIME TO ZONE TIME

Greenwich Mean Time kept on a 24-hour-dial navigation watch, can be converted to zone time that we use every day by applying our particular zone correction to Greenwich Mean Time. For example, assume that we are in Eastern Standard Time, Zone 5. In west longitude, we would simply subtract 5 hours from the Greenwich Mean Time to have Eastern Standard Time. If we were in east longitude, we ould add the zone. To convert zone time to Greenwich Mean Time, we would add the zone in west gitude and subtract it in east longitude.

he foregoing example applies to the relationship between Greenwich Mean Time and to the time kept over the entire Eastern Standard Time Zone. A number of different kinds of time and complex adaptations of such times used in navigation would require

numerous pages to explain. And since they are not
particularly pertinent to the simpler approach used
in this book, they are omitted except those already
utilized in the foregoing text. If the reader is concerned about time conversions and how he can use
Greenwich Mean Time in the few simple examples
given herein, he can have someone familiar with the
subject set his 24-hour watch to Greenwich Mean
Time to give him this watch time continually. For
practice he should then compare Greenwich Mean
Time with Standard Time.

CORRECT GREENWICH MEAN TIME

As we read books on navigation, we see a great
deal of emphasis on chronometer (watch or clock)
correction. With a small transistor radio having short-
wave bands, we can, under most circumstances and
unless we fail to get a time signal, disregard the time
correction given in various manuals. To determine
the exact moment of Greenwich Mean Time, a sextant sight is best aided by using a stopwatch along
with the 24-hour-dial watch.

The method used for getting the exact second of
time by the stopwatch is to select and record an
exact advance moment of time from the Greenwich
Mean Time 24-hour-dial watch and to start the stopwatch when the 24-hour watch reaches that moment.
Keep the stopwatch running up to the exact moment
of making the sight and then trip it. Add the elapsed
time indicated on the stopwatch to the moment of
time selected from the 24-hour watch. This gives the
exact moment of the sextant sight. For example, if
you selected the advance time of 03 hours and 20

minutes from the 24-hour Greenwich Mean Time watch on which to start the stopwatch and tripped it 18 seconds later, at the moment of taking the altitude sight, the moment of taking the sight would simply be 03 hours, 20 minutes, 18 seconds.

CORRECT DATE

The date used in navigational astronomy is always the Greenwich date. We should be careful of this date, because a sight made on Polaris at 9 P.M., Central Standard Time, June 10, for example, would be 3 hours Greenwich Mean Time, June 11. You see, 6 hours have elapsed since it was 9 P.M. at Greenwich, carrying into the next day. (See the use of Greenwich Mean Time in the *Nautical Almanac*.)

DETERMINING THE DATE WITH A SEXTANT SIGHT ON THE SUN

Unless a constant diary is kept in the wilderness, we are apt to lose track of the date. The date is important when making sextant sights for latitude and longitude, as described in Chapter 8, and of course we need it for the daily record of events. In determining the date with a sextant, the only important facts we need to know are the approximate latitude of our position and the sun's declination.

Procedure

With a sextant we take a sight on the sun at high noon for altitude when the sun is on the meridian, as we did for latitude in Chapter 8. When the sun is

north of the equator and we are north of the sun,
we subtract the corrected altitude of the sun from
90 degrees to obtain our zenith distance. Then we
merely subtract the zenith distance in degrees and
minutes from our known latitude in degrees and
minutes, to obtain the declination of the sun for high
noon on the day of observation. If now we open the
Nautical Almanac to the nearest estimated date, we
will find on one of the sun-column pages a declination figure that corresponds with the declination we
obtained from our sextant sight on the sun. The particular daily page that carries this corresponding
declination is, of course, our proper date.

There are three variations of our own position in
relation to the sun's position north or south of the
equator that need to be considered when determining
the date: when the equator is between the sun and
our position; when the sun is between the equator
and our position; and when our position is between
the equator and the sun. In each case we first determine the zenith distance as we did in the foregoing
example.

1. When the equator is between the sun and our
   position, then zenith distance minus our latitude equals the sun's declination; or, 90 degrees minus corrected meridian altitude, minus
   our latitude equals declination.

2. When the sun is between the equator and our
   position, then our latitude minus zenith distance
   equals the sun's declination; or, 90 degrees
   minus corrected meridian altitude, subtracted
   from our latitude equals declination.

3. When our position is between the equator and

the sun, then zenith distance plus our latitude equals the sun's declination; or, 90 degrees minus corrected meridian altitude, plus our latitude equals declination.

TIME OF DAY WITH A SEXTANT SIGHT

Besides the date, correct time of day can also be had with a sextant sight on the sun or other body by working a single H.O. 214 latitude line of position backward. We must know our exact latitude and longitude for this problem. An outline for the H.O. 214 method in working a line-of-position solution is given later in this appendix. With shortwave radio available for time signals, the H.O. 214 reversal computation to find time has, however, been omitted in this brief volume.

INDEX CORRECTION OF SEXTANT

Sometimes through lack of perfect adjustment there is a small index error in a sextant that must be added or subtracted, as the case may be, for the measured altitude. The important thing is to know if such an error does exist in the instrument and whether the error is plus or minus from a true reading. Sextant error can be checked by taking a noon latitude sight at a known latitude and the amount of plus or minus error noted. It is well to take a number of such sights at the known latitude position in order to obtain an average for a more accurate knowledge of the error. A plus or minus sextant reading from the true one will show your position to be either north or south of the known latitude position of the sight. There can also be a bubble error, which should be checked and corrected on some reference-datum point, determined by a transit level or from a very low sextant observation point sighted on a sea or lake horizon. Instruments having these errors should be adjusted on the sextant itself by a capable instrument man, or a plus or minus allowance should be made, as the case may be, when computing all sights.

SERVICING THE BUBBLE SEXTANT

Xylene, a highly volatile fluid used in reservoirs of bubble sextants, will evaporate in time. This is an inexpensive liquid that must be ordered by a retail druggist from a wholesale drug-supply house, because it is not an item generally retailed. Merely remove the screw filler plug from the bubble-assembly reservoir and fill the chamber through a small refill hole, using a hypodermic syringe and needle. (Do not use a plastic syringe, since Xylene will dissolve the plastic.) Keep sextants or transits well protected in travel. These are instruments of great precision, and though they are fairly rugged, they will not stand too much abuse even when encased.

USING THE SEXTANT FOR TRIANGULATION

Earlier, reference was made to the use of a compact explorer's transit, or theodolite, on expeditions for triangulation lines of position to islands, points, mountain peaks, and so on, for fixing a position. The sextant, while not having the convenience of the transit for these horizontal angles, can be improvised for triangulation work by removing the bubble as heretofore described and turning the sextant on its side. It can then be made to measure horizontal instead of the regular vertical angles for which it is designed. Since the sextant, unlike the transit, does not have a magnetic compass, the bearing to an island, point, or mountain peak is first accurately determined with a separate compass sight, then the horizontal angle between the compass line and other point is measured with the sextant for the true bearing. Both compass and sextant observations are best made when these instruments are used on a tripod or other improvised support.

Besides measuring the elevations of celestial bodies as we have done in obtaining our latitude, the sextant can also be used in computing the height of terrestrial objects such as mountains, mesas, etc., for identification or research. The methods are given in any book on geometry, and therefore need not be described here.

CONVERSION OF TIME INTO ARC

24 hours of time	= 360 degrees of arc (longitude)
1 hour of time	= 15 degrees of arc (longitude)
1 minute of time	= 15 minutes of arc (longitude)
1 second of time	= 15 seconds of arc (longitude)

Longitude, thus, can be expressed in both arc or

time. (See the *Nautical Almanac* or the free sur-
veyor's *Ephemeris* booklets for various conversion
tables.)

ALTITUDE CORRECTIONS

In Chapter 8 the altitude corrections for refraction (errors caused by the bending of light rays) of
both the sun and the Pole Star were, for convenience
and simplicity in the examples given, referred to the
star table on the inside cover of the *Nautical Almanac*. This star-refraction table is applicable to the
sun, as well, when using the bubble sextant and when
the bubble-type sextant and the marine-type sextant
are used in combination with a mercury-pool artificial horizon, because the *center* of the sun automati-
cally becomes the focus of altitude when measured
by these methods.

The marine-type sextant works in such a way that
when the sun or star is properly indexed in the
instrument by a combination of split-view mirror,
prism, and scope, the lower rim of the sun appears to
be touching the horizon, that is, tangent with it. In
fact, the sun though well up in the sky, seems about
to set.

At sea, on a large lake, or from the shore of such
water, therefore, when using the sextant for a sight
on the sun, the lower rim of the sun is brought in
contact with the visible water horizon. Correction
then must be referred to the *sun table* on the inside
cover of the *Almanac*—not to the star table, as we
did with the bubble sextant. You can see that in
using the sea horizon on the sun's lower rim, our
altitude would be in error the difference between the

sun's lower rim and the sun's center. For example: If the sextant altitude of the sun was, say, 36 degrees and 20 minutes to the lower rim, the correction from the lower rim to the center, as given in the sun table, would be 15 minutes of arc. This added to our sextant altitude would give us a corrected altitude to the center of the sun of 36 degrees, 35 minutes. When using the natural horizon, one must also take into consideration the height of the sextant above the water level, called "height of eye correction." This correction can be had at a glance from a table on the inside cover of the *Nautical Almanac*. It is a subtractive correction.

ILLUMINATION OF THE BUBBLE SEXTANT

Bubble sextants for night work are equipped with standard flashlight dry cells, with built-in electric bulbs for illuminating the index, and with "grain of wheat" bulbs for illuminating the bubble when sighting on a star. Batteries should be removed and stored separately when the sextant is not being used for long periods of time to prevent acid-leak corrosion. Also, remove the bulbs from time to time and clean up the electric contact points, since a slight corrosion takes place from the galvanic action of one kind of metal upon another.

MAGNETIZING THE COMPASS NEEDLE

If a compass needle becomes sluggish by having lost all or part of its magnetism, it can easily be remagnetized by one of several methods. The most convenient for the average user is to remove the

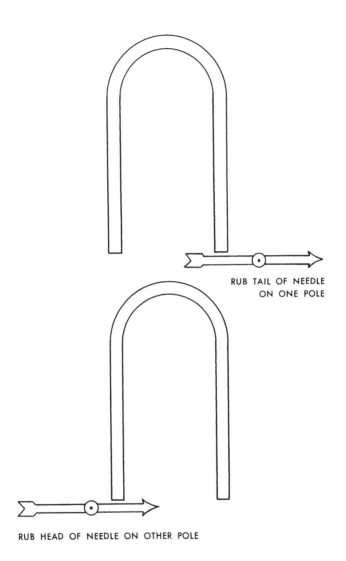

RUB TAIL OF NEEDLE
ON ONE POLE

RUB HEAD OF NEEDLE ON OTHER POLE

FIG. 56 *Remagnetizing the Compass Needle*

needle and remagnetize it with the poles of an ordinary horseshoe-type magnet. The method is shown in the accompanying illustration.

Rub each half of the needle, as shown, in one direction only. This requires but a minute or two for full charge.

If the polarity of the needle becomes reversed by your having confused the poles, the polarity can be corrected at once by switching the poles of the magnet on the needle and repeating the rubbing operation. Another method for remagnetizing a needle is to place it in a cardboard tube around which a number of copper-wire wrappings have been made; in short, an improvised, hollow, electric coil. By attaching one end of the coil wire to a terminal of a storage battery (6- or 12-volt) and merely "sparking" the other end of the coil wire on the opposite terminal a few times, the needle lying inside the coil will become magnetized. Here, too, check the polarity for proper direction. If the polarity of the needle is reversed, change the needle direction in the tube, "spark" again, and it will be corrected.

ALTITUDE

Altitude is the angular elevation or angular distance of a celestial body above the horizon, measured in degrees, minutes, and seconds of arc. Angular terminology has been avoided in this book for utter simplicity, but it is easily understood if we consider that the center of the earth is the focal point and that lines drawn from this point to the sun and stars and from this point through our own position create an angle. Where these lines from the earth's center break the surface of the earth, they give us positions on the earth's surface relative to one another. We can assume this center-of-the-earth hypothesis for working angles, because the earth is but a tiny point in relation to the distant stars.

AZIMUTH

Azimuth, as used in navigation, is the direction of a celestial body from the observer. H.O. 214 navigation tables show azimuth in degrees and tenths of a degree, tabulated as Azimuth 94.7°, and so on. Converted to degrees and minutes, this would read: 94° 42'.

BEARING

Bearing is the angle between a line connecting two points and a north-south line or meridian. Azimuth and bearing are sometimes used interchangeably, but bearing is usually considered to be the horizontal direction of one terrestrial point from another. Azimuth most often has referred to the direction of celestial bodies. We now have come to use azimuth as any direction from 0 to 360 degrees, while bearing has come to be regarded as a direction determined by quadrant calibration. (See Quadrant Calibration, pages 197-199.)

DECLINATION

Declination of a celestial body is its latitude. In the *Nautical Almanac,* declinations are marked N and S to show whether the body is north or south of the equator. Plus or minus signs show which direction the sun in its north and south annual movement is traveling. The amount of its movement can be determined by comparing declination figures in the *Almanac* from one hour or day to another. Its hourly change north or south varies from about one minute of latitude during its greatest movement late in March and September to nothing late in June and December. For convenience and utility, we call the sun's movement its "apparent" movement, because actually it is the earth which moves in relation to the sun. (Declination here pertains to celestial bodies, not to compass declination.)

DEGREES

Degrees, minutes, and seconds of arc are expressed, for example, as $42° 23' 07''$, or its approximate rougher equivalent in degrees and decimals: $42.4°$.

GREENWICH HOUR ANGLE (GHA) OF A CELESTIAL BODY

Greenwich Hour Angle (GHA) of a celestial body expressed in nontechnical language is its longitude measured westward from the meridian of Greenwich, in degrees, minutes, and seconds of arc, from $0°$ to $360°$. GHA, as stated, is analogous to longitude, except that longitude is measured east and west from the meridian of Greenwich to $180°$, while the Greenwich Hour Angle is always figured westward from $0°$ to $360°$ (see Longitude). Some navigators of late have preferred to treat longitude in the same manner as hour angle, measuring it westward from 0° to 360°. This possibly gains something toward simplicity and in time may catch on, especially if enough general, authoritative approval can be had.

LATITUDE

Latitude is measured in degrees, minutes, and seconds of arc from the equator, north and south to the geographical poles. The equator is at zero degrees; the earth's poles at 90 degrees. One minute of latitude is equal to one nautical mile, 6080 feet. A statute or regular mile being 5280 feet, 6.6 nautical miles equal 7.6 statute miles.

LONGITUDE

Longitude is measured in degrees, minutes, and seconds, east and west from the meridian of Greenwich, which is zero degrees, to the International Date Line, which is 180 degrees, where, contrary to the literary romance of old, that "never the twain shall meet," as one authority proclaimed, "east and west do meet." (See Greenwich Hour Angle.) One minute of longitude is equal to one nautical mile at the equator and decreases to nothing at the North and South Poles.

ARIES, OR FIRST POINT OF ARIES (VERNAL EQUINOX)

In this appendix a method is given for finding the latitude line of position from a sight on the Pole Star at any time that the star is visible. The Greenwich

Hour Angle of Aries is required for this. Briefly, Aries can be defined as a reference point on the celestial sphere from which we measure westward the hour angle of the stars. The resulting measurement is called the Sidereal Hour Angle (SHA), a component used in obtaining the hour angle of stars. For greater simplicity, where any of the information in this volume is concerned, an understanding of the definition of Aries and Sidereal Hour Angle can, if desired, be disregarded without impairing the end results in the methods given.

QUADRANT CALIBRATION

In Chapter 4, reference is made to quadrant calibration of the magnetic compass. It is a rather unique system that has for many years lent itself well to surveying; the magnetic compasses which are built into transits are provided with this calibration system. Recently, quadrant calibration has been added to various compasses—even the sportsman's—in addition to their own various conventional calibration systems. Some navigators are now finding it more convenient to use the quadrant system of calibration for setting off the azimuths (directions) of celestial bodies. On the whole, the system promises to have increasing, universal approval for all directional needs. The calibration is very easy to understand, once it is examined. I think you will like it.

Note in the illustration that the circle, which simulates a compass dial, is divided into quarters, or quadrants. The quadrants are numbered 1 to 4, counterclockwise, beginning with the upper right

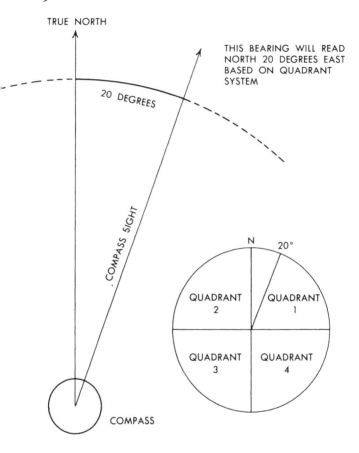

FIG. 57 *Bearing (Direction) by Quadrant Calibration*

quadrant. Each quadrant is separately calibrated in degrees from o to 90, beginning at both the north and south zero points of the compass dial, and numbering east and west to 90 degrees.

While any degree of the 90 in each of the quadrants can be a particular bearing to a distant point, four basic examples only are given in the illustration. After compass declination has been applied in the usual manner, as treated in Chapter 4, and the lubber's line or the compass sight has been trained on a chosen distant objective, the method of reading the bearing will be, for example: "north 15 degrees east" or "south 15 degrees west," whatever the bearing from any quadrant happens to be.

The reader will by now have discovered an extremely interesting aspect of this calibration method: By using both cardinal points and degrees in the reading of each bearing, a better mental picture of the direction is had at once.

COMPASS ACCURACY

While the magnetic compass has been in use for surveying and other directional functions and has proved quite practical, we should bear in mind that the magnetic compass is not the precise instrument we would like it to be. Variation has been given in Chapter 4, but we should recognize that some unstable variation of the compass is possible not only from place to place but even from one part of the day to the other, and many distracting influences affect accuracy of the magnetic compass. For extremely accurate bearings in exploration work and surveys, observations should be made with a transit on the sun or stars. (See Polar Distance in this appendix.) However, this instability of the magnetic compass does not apply in most ordinary, routine travel afield and need not be disconcerting in our route-finding program if the declination of the compass and serious magnetic disturbances are always considered and each bearing is taken with care.

THE ASTROCOMPASS (SOLAR COMPASS)

The astrocompass does not have a magnetic needle but is used to find our direction by sighting on any celestial body. Latitude, declination, and local hour angle are required for the sight. Local hour angle is obtained by subtracting the observer's longitude from the Greenwich Hour Angle in west longitude and by adding this longitude in east longitude. The astrocompass is first leveled by two built-in levels. Observer's latitude, declination, and local hour angle of the body are then set on the respective scales. A sight on the body following these settings will orient the instrument to proper directions. In using the sun with this instrument, a shadow falling between two lines is employed to avoid sighting into the sun's glare (see Fig. 24).

THE TRANSIT OR THEODOLITE

The transit, or theodolite, in the simplest sense, is an instrument mounted on a tripod for measuring both horizontal and vertical angles. It is provided with a built-in magnetic compass for determining bearings (directions), or without a compass for bearings from celestial bodies, and with a telescope for sighting these various horizontal bearings and vertical angles. It has a level for use as an artificial horizon in measuring the altitude of a celestial body or a terrestrial elevation. It can be used to great advantage in measuring the horizontal angles of triangulation described in Chapter 5, and it will also do the job of the sextant when it can be set on solid ground or on ice. This is the instrument we see mounted on a tripod from time to time on highways and during land surveys. In the wilderness a smaller and more compact transit is used for greatest portability.

CONVENTIONAL NAVIGATION METHODS

THE H.O. 214 METHOD OF FIXING ONE'S POSITION

No effort has been made in this volume to include conventional navigation methods; but, no doubt, some readers will want to explore this field.

The convenient H.O. 214 conventional line-of-position method for fixing an exact position has rapidly become the most popular. A brief outline of this method will follow. While these conventional H.O. 214 and other methods are much longer and more involved than the selected short methods given in this volume, as will be apparent by the outline, the H.O. 214 method requires only common arithmetic. The method itself will readily be grasped by anyone keeping his wits about him.

The trigonometry once required for solutions of the spherical triangle, which was such mathematical labor in earlier years and which was essential to working a celestial line of position, has now with the advent of the H.O. 214 tables been reduced to handy tabulated solutions, available from the Government Hydrographic Office. The following publications and items of equipment are needed for an understanding and working of this H.O. 214 method:

Nautical Almanac—$3.50 (British and American
        publications are identical).

H.O. 214 Computed Altitude and Azimuth Tables,
        selected for proper range of
        latitudes traveled; issued in 9
        volumes from 0° to 90°, each
        volume covering 10° of lati-
        tude. $3.75 per volume.

H.O. 214 form sheets for tabulating solution en-
        tries (low-cost item).

Mercator chart plotting sheets for proper latitude
        (low-cost item).

(The above publications, forms, and charts are
available upon order from the Superintendent of
Documents, U.S. Government Printing Office, Washington, D.C. 20402.)

Bubble or marine-type sextant, or explorer's tran-
        sit (a large supply of bubble
        sextants has been released
        through surplus channels and
        may be bought at 10 per cent
        of their original cost to the
        government).

Artificial horizon (for use on land only with a
        marine or bubble sextant. Can
        be made at home. See Figure
        46B).

Watch (one with a 24-hour dial set to keep Green-
        wich Mean Time).

Radio (small, portable, transistor-type with short-wave bands for obtaining accurate government time signals. A length of fine stranded wire [about 50 to 100 feet] with a small insulator on each end should be included for an auxiliary, overhead wilderness antenna. One end can be tied with a cord to the branch of a tree or suspended from a tent pole. Height usually increases the quality of the signal).

Dividers

Protractor (10- or 12-inch)

Lead pencils (hard and soft), eraser, pen knife, and a small piece of fine sandpaper, or small, fine file for keeping pencils well pointed.

A Brief Outline of the Steps in the H.O. 214 Method

1. Measure the altitude of the body with a sextant.
2. Note the exact moment of Greenwich Mean Time when the sight is made.
3. Correct the altitude for refraction.
4. Enter the *Nautical Almanac* or the *Air Almanac* with the exact time of the sight and take out the Greenwich Hour Angle and the declination of the body for this moment of time.

5. Assume the nearest longitude—one that when subtracted from or added to the Greenwich Hour Angle will give a result in whole degrees (subtracted if the observer is west of Greenwich, added if east of Greenwich).

6. Assume the nearest latitude that will be in whole degrees.

7. Enter the H.O. 214 tables at the page of assumed latitude under the column of the nearest declination. Opposite the local hour angle select the tabulated altitude, Δd correction, and azimuth. (Watch the heading of the declination pages—whether the same or contrary name to the assumed latitude.)

8. Find the Δd correction from the multiplication table inside the back cover of the H.O. 214 tables.

9. Add the Δd correction to the tabulated altitude if the altitude is increasing as the tabulated declination approached the exact declination; subtract the Δd correction if the altitude is decreasing as the tabulated declination approached the exact declination. The result is the computed altitude, or what it would be at the assumed position. (The corrections used in the above steps are also described in the H.O. 214 tables.)

10. From the above, the position is plotted on a Mercator chart, several graphic examples of such plots being given in the volumes of H.O. 214 tables.

11. Compare the measured, corrected altitude

with the computed altitude. The resulting difference is called the intercept, being the difference on the plotted azimuth line between the assumed position and the actual one.

Unfortunately, most books on navigation, if I am to judge by complaints from aspiring laymen, are written by instructors talking to instructors, rather than by instructors carefully, step by step, guiding the uninformed. The most valiant effort in describing the H.O. 214 method that I have found to reach the student without basic navigational knowledge is contained in a small paperback book written by the late M. R. Hart, *How to Navigate Today,* recently revised by W. A. McEwan (Cornell Maritime Press, Cambridge, Mass. $2.25). It deals only with celestial navigation and not with position finding generally.

Sooner or later, the student interested in navigational astronomy will, of course, want to acquire the 1500-page tome *American Practical Navigator H.O. Publication Number 9,* originally by Bowditch ($6.25); the 700-page *Air Navigation H.O. Publication 216* ($7.50); and other subsequent publications available from the U.S. Government Printing Office and private publishers. *H.O. Publications Number 9* and *216* do not provide a systematic, gradual, step-by-step course of celestial navigation instruction, but they do contain a vast and valuable categorical knowledge.

Investment in these volumes will be worthwhile at first for reference and the glossary of navigation terms they provide. Later they will supply basic material for continuing study. Unique, highly informative charts on star finding are contained in these volumes.

Some universities and colleges offer short night courses on navigational astronomy. Once a fair grasp of the fundamentals of the subject is had, no study can compare with diligent practice in the field—and so, *Bon Voyage!*

INDEX

Calvin Rutstrum (1895–1982) was one of the best-known outdoorsmen of his generation and the author of more than a dozen books on wilderness travel and technique. In the 1960s, he enjoyed a wide following as interest in outdoor adventure boomed. Today he is known by canoe country aficionados who are fascinated by the lore and romance of canoe travel and wilderness adventure.